20/twenty Publishing

USA

2015

Cover credit: 20/twenty Publishing

Illustrations by Gerald Olesker

ISBN 978-1523775378 (PBK)

www.jeffkleid.com

Email: info@jeffkleid.com

Printed in the United States of America

FOREWARD

Networking is one of the greatest tools to build relationships and ultimately grow a business. Networking, however, is not easy for many. It is important to be able to engage and develop relationships with others. With his creative play on Texas Hold'em, Jeff Kleid teaches the reader to work with their own 'deck of cards' when forging relationships and building connections.

Networking is often perceived as a transaction, but if, instead, it is done with genuine intent to learn and grow, it can yield fantastic success both personally and professionally. Jeff lends a fantastic spin to an 'old school' business topic. He makes the act of networking more engaging. When you are aware of whom you are and the hand you were dealt, you can more easily interact and engage with others. With the strategies in this book, you can more effectively leverage your style to yield success. Jeff will help you make networking work and encourages you to have fun in the process!

This fantastic author can be confident that readers will have gained a broader perspective of the discipline of networking as a result of his efforts in this easy-to-read and engaging book. Whether you're a veteran, in the military, an entrepreneur, a Real Estate Agent, or looking to grow your book of business in the corporate world, the tools in this book will serve you well. As CEO of a company that offers legal business solutions for business owners, I am confident that entrepreneurs of all experience levels will find Jeff's take on networking to be a welcome guide toward greater success. I am looking forward to sharing this with our clients as they look to protect, grow and build their businesses.

Deborah Sweeney
CEO
MyCorporation.com

Networking
with
The Cards
You Are Dealt

Jeff Kleid

Contents

No turning back.
Managing relationships within the clients network
Slow play.
What are your hot buttons or what excites you?
EXERCISE
Is anyone dropping out?
Find a Champion.
Think about and compare a direct sales experience
with an indirect sales experience through
Networking. EXERCISE

Should we split the pot?
River – fifth and last community card dealt face up.
What a game changer.
The strategies of the game.
How do you bet when different cards come up?
How do I decide the best use of my time?
All About you. EXERCISE
I am still here, now what?
Why should you stay in the game, but not in the
hand? EXERCISE
Why did I keep a seat at the table?

Online Poker – Social Media
Take a look at a Real Estate Agent.
For Facebook Networking 101, know the following?
How do you use Twitter to Network?

I may go all in.
Going all in.
Why do you need a seat at the table?
How do I make this hand work?

Acknowledgements

To Wendy, Joey and Robbie,
Rona, Debbie, Cindy and Mike
Randy W, Tony C, Steve E, Scott L, Pat H, Skene B, Chuck L,
Dale S, Jeremy G, Gerald O, Vince I, Tim E, John S, Greg H, Ron B

Networking involves a series of different strategies. For the purpose of the book we follow Texas Hold'em as a guide to understanding those different strategies.

The key components to Texas Hold'em which continue throughout are:

The two cards that are dealt.

The Flop – three cards dealt face up

The Turn – one card dealt face up

And the River – one last card dealt face up.

At the end of the game your best hand will use 5 out of the 7 cards.

While it is possible to win a hand by everybody folding in poker, for the sake of this book and the educational value of the strategies, think of each interaction as a different hand and that you are simultaneously playing multiple hands at once.

Each time you are in a new hand, you will have to adjust how you play.

Now we can get into how you can Network.

Dedicated to those gone too soon

My Dad, Harvey, Thom M, Craig M, Steve F,
Hideo A, Mike H, Allan G

INTRODUCTION

What am I writing about?

For the last twenty plus years I have watched my wife read novel after novel, day-by-day. On a regular basis, I have sat around the table with people raving about books they read, that they felt were life changing. In both instances I have always wondered why I don't have the same passion or get that same feeling about reading, or more specifically, reading business or self-help books. Quite possibly, my apathy towards reading those types of books may have limited my success. I will never know, I just don't or didn't find the right rhythm for reading books that would help me get there. With that said, ironically, here I am writing a book, in the hopes that you will find a nugget or something that helps guide you and makes you more successful in a direction that you are trying to go. I am not writing this book thinking that it will be your AHA moment and change your life, I am however hopeful that you learn how to use a skill or find at least something useful that relates to you and will help guide you. If you walk away understanding whom you are, what you're capable of and what you can do for yourself to get to another level, then I will have succeeded.

I am writing this book about networking, not a transaction or a sale, but rather a lifestyle whether for business or pleasure. We all do it, sometimes we need someone to put an objective spin on what we are doing so we can become better at it and do it with a purpose.

Why am I writing this?

I've spent so many years being the beneficiary of so many good people; have surpassed success I could only imagine. While fully cognizant that there are several others with greater success both financially and personally than myself, in my book, knowing where and how I started to where I got to, I will take it any day of the week. I also find it helpful to stop, take a breath, look back and look forward acknowledging that I did not do it all by myself but rather in concert with several great people and interactions throughout. As I sit around a table talking

1

with people as a mentor or walk through the process of growing my current business venture with my partner, I know I have something to share and I believe there is something for everyone. However, though I am convinced there is value in this book, I cannot say for sure that there is value for you. Nevertheless, I am firmly convinced that the time is now for me to write this for you.

It's funny, one day I was sitting in a business forum I have been a part of for over 12 years. It is a group of business owners with whom I regularly discuss the good, bad and the ugly of running a business. At one point I was talking about why I was writing this, and one of the guys said it seems like an ego thing, and my response was that this book was something that had to be written and the story of networking had to be told. Next, another guy at the table said, " Who do you think you are? Kanye?"

Clearly if you aren't focused on the current music scene you may not be familiar with Kanye West, but if you are, you understand the comment to mean something to the effect that I believe everyone wants to hear what I have to say. My response to that is that I may not view Kanye as the guy I need to listen to, but he has so many fans and followers there must be something he is doing that gets him that reaction. So Kanye, if you are reading this and feel the need to brush up on your networking skills, please let me know your thoughts on the book. Fact is, I think I owe it to myself to spend time educating others with what I have learned along the way. Hopefully others, yourself included, will see a value for you, in your world. And that would be great.

I ask the same question to so many people: what have they done lately to help someone? I have specifically said the help has to be measurable and can't be monetary. Guess what, from the answers I've received, it's pretty clear that very few people can separate those two as functions. Hopefully this book will help with that.

I can't speak to why I am fascinated by poker or for that matter Craps, Dice, Blackjack, etc. whatever game you have to think at to understand, but in some cases you may not even change the outcome. I chose Texas Hold'em and poker largely because of the strategies of how you bet, follow the game, into the river, weave and wind throughout the process to get to the end of the game. I don't think of this as gambling, I focus instead on the strategy throughout the process. Again, it doesn't matter what level you play it at, except for the fact that when people play at the lower levels or even in tournament style play they tend not to follow a strategy of the game or truly understand the different strategies of the game, which can make it harder for you to play in a fashion that yields statistical results. The goal is to up your game at every level, regardless of what that means for you.

It doesn't necessarily mean you have to consistently move up in your job position, or you're making more money. What it does mean is that you are constantly challenged or feel engaged. Hopefully your task at hand is constantly making you better. That is kind of the premise of switching from a low limit table to a high limit table; it shouldn't be about the level of money you make. At least for me it becomes about the commitment level and understanding what the other players at the table know about the game. They understand how to give a referral, take a referral and service a client. Or they understand what needs to be done to accomplish the task or goal they set out to accomplish if it is not business related.

As their game gets better it makes you adjust yours regularly. By no means should this be taken as a sign to move away from players at a lower table, associates, friends, clients, etc., but rather embrace additional relationships who you can better assist and be a trusted advisor or source for. You do this so it raises your world and how it benefits them and you.

Throughout Facebook and other Social Networks, emails, phone calls, and so forth I am constantly engaged with people from my youth, high school, college, business, charity, etc. It is a very diverse group of people that I have met through all these walks of life. Some haven't changed, others have truly excelled, or perhaps I've met them in recent years and they are already established. Regardless of the who, the how and the why, these relationships may not have any value as I move through life, but as a memory the relationship continues and in some cases has moved forward into the next phase of the game. It may be no different than that chocolate ice cream you ate at the Sugar Bowl in Scottsdale when you were a kid and having it again thirty years later, all those memories rush back and instantly you are in that moment, or maybe you have that interaction and several others in between so it becomes a memory and possibility for a new memory to be made. It's ok to have those.

This book came out of several interactions networking with others. I have been growing a new company in real estate and lending, interacting with both new and old relationships. These either became personal relationships or good business relationships who understand my commitment to how I conduct business. Throughout those many interactions I realized I started teaching others the secrets of my success and how my networking interactions helped get me there. Of course, we can't forget about the failures in the mix as well. At the same time I realized it's those interactions that not everyone understands. After several months of these interactions and then giving a handful of presentations I felt I had to continue this journey of sharing and targeted specific groups who I think may gain from someone else's direct view on adjusting to the business and networking world and need a little help getting to the next level to provide for themselves and their families. Since I have been fortunate to learn so much from others, sharing my insight just makes sense. Whether you are a returning veteran, divorced, widowed, new in business, back in business, or just trying to make new relationships, this book is for you. I set out to create a book that adds value; hopefully it will do that for you.

Bottom Up

What does networking look like from the bottom up? Most people hear the term networking and instantly freeze up, come up with excuses and find reasons why it doesn't work for them. At the same time, they see someone and their success in the same environment they are or want to be in and they are a bit jealous and want to be like that person. In reality we need to understand our limits, struggles, abilities, etc. Who you are, how you are, what do you need, and how can you get it are really the questions that most of us have on a daily basis, focused on it or not, that is what it comes down to. LinkedIn for example, was a top down approach to networking, in which high-level executives, CEO's, business coaches, venture capital folks and entrepreneurs communicated. I am a big proponent of them, I myself have been a member of a high level forum since the early 2000s but with that said, as a service provider who happened to start in sales and build a couple of companies to some significant success, I also have that service background that helps me to understand the front lines from the bottom up. That's where this book is focused, starting at the boots on the ground level, and it starts with you, your abilities and your level of comfort. The goal is that at whatever level you feel you are able to address your needs; something in this book should be able to assist you. Focusing on the bottom up approach is not about being a superstar, hitting homeruns every day. It's about engaging in whatever environment you are in or have to put yourself in on a daily basis.

Whether you are in business to be in business, wholesale, service, retail, manufacturing, on the dock, whatever it is, you need to understand the basics of networking and communication. If you have gotten this far and are still reading, this book should help you get to that next level. If I wasn't afforded a seat at the table or assisted with opportunities by the few people who gave them to me along the way I wouldn't understand the mechanics that I do. Sometimes, I get sidetracked and pay attention to the fact that maybe I should never have had some of the opportunities that I have or have been fortunate enough to run with. The moment is usually a fleeting one, as in reality, while we may not choose the cards we are dealt, there is always a way to make them work.

I didn't set out to be an entrepreneur, I didn't even set out to be a business owner. In fact, my view on business ownership was the struggle I constantly saw from my parents through running their own business and quite frankly it wasn't that great, it never was a success. It was a struggle, a sacrifice, and definitely life changing for my family and me. I didn't set out to be anything other than a guy who paid his bills and lived life. Somewhere along the line through all that knowledge and understanding ultimately exactly what I have become is an entrepreneur, a networking expert and a businessman with a zest for success only in that it has given me the ability to provide for my family and at the same time enjoy quality time with my family and friends. So, hopefully your take away from the bottom up will take you where you need to go.

Prior to the Buy In

What am I trying to accomplish?

Once you find the nugget within the book don't stop there, because this book is less about me telling you how great I am at networking and more about you gaining some knowledge that helps guide you to the end of your game. Now, I am going to share with you the way the book ends. (Spoiler Alert) It ends with you in the middle of a game.

The idea is that through this process you will learn that networking is a continuous journey and that is what makes it so unique and different from selling. You can buy leads. Contact old clients, ask for three referrals, all of the things that people profess will make you successful, but with networking you create an ecosystem that does all of the above for you.

I won't say Networking is harder work than selling, I will say it is more of a commitment to a process rather than a sale of a product. For thousands of years people have been networking to keep their own personal worlds and the world in general moving.

Think of all the people throughout history good or bad who gave away something first in order to get what they needed or wanted to get them to the next level. Think of Oskar Schindler from the movie Schindler's List. A sad movie yes, but quite inspiring and if you think back to the beginning of the movie, Oskar Schindler went all in, figuring out what the Germans needed in order to get his work force. He bought bottles of Scotch, threw lavish parties, sent great gifts, he created a great feeling for others while he worked his way through the crowd to get what he needed to create a work force for himself. Clearly, his motives changed in the middle of the story, but again he then used that same network for the good of a people at a huge risk to himself. In both instances he was networking even if the original premise was to stuff his coffers. Schindler genuinely learned about his employees and wanted to help them with their plight. He knew who was at his table, understood their needs and how to play the game.

There are so many hands, that patience truly is a virtue in poker and the same goes for networking. It's very simple; it is the law of large numbers and yes there is always that one that gets away.

EXERCISE

What should you think about when finding the right network?

1. What am I trying to accomplish?
2. What am I trying to sell?
3. Who am I trying to meet?
4. What is my timeframe for making the right connection?
5. How much time do I need to spend daily, weekly, and monthly networking?
6. Do I want to be here for myself or did someone else tell me to attend?

Helpful Hint: There is no wrong answer, but planning ahead with time, and whether or not you really want to be there will help you know which group is right for you. Depending on your answers, different groups may be a better fit for your situation.

Back to the Basics

How do you know you are in the right place? Any time we step out of our comfort zone we aren't sure we are in the right place. It may sound strange, but you will know it when you find it. The hard part is that you may find the right fit, but for the wrong reason. While on its face there is nothing wrong with that, I found a great group that I truly enjoyed being a part of and it made a difference in several individuals' lives by helping them get through Cal State Northridge on scholarships. Problem for me was that I had a young family and realized as much as I felt good about helping these kids it wasn't a big enough help to justify the time I was taking from my own family.

One of the first things to remember about networking is your relationships, regardless of whether they are good or they are bad, yes, the world is really small. I remember my first job when I moved to California; I worked at the Red Lion in Costa Mesa as a waiter. In a very short time I had a small following of regulars, but a couple months later I realized it wasn't for me. So I moved on. A few years later I was applying to be a bartender at a couple of places locally in Orange County and met with a manager who was interviewing me. I immediately recognized him as one of those regulars. Of course being such a short stint at Red Lion I left it off my resume, but clearly he noticed. Needless to say I did not get the job, but you get the moral of the story. Just in case, understand you never know under what circumstances you will meet up with someone again so make your impression count.

EXERCISE:

List the 5 things you would like to be better at when networking.

1.
2.
3.
4.
5.

How have you missed an opportunity because of the above?

What are some ways you could handle it differently in the future?

Helpful Hint: Sometimes accepting the things we are not able to do is just as important as what we would like to do better. I accept that I am not a polished speaker and used to get frustrated at meetings and events when my elevator pitch wasn't as polished. I adapted my elevator pitch to be who I am.

Chapter 1

What excites me?
Why this Book and Why Now?

Everyone has in them an opportunity to build a great network, but that doesn't mean who, what, how or why that network will come into existence or will be beneficial. Even after reading this book and doing some of the exercises you may not figure out the value of your network or how to use it. You may have more work ahead of you, and that's ok. I didn't know or understand my network or how to use it or how it used me until I really started to see the mechanics of the way my past has intertwined with itself into my present and most likely will in my future.

Here is what I do know about myself. I know that not everybody is going to have my skills, not everybody is going to understand how I think, and I definitely know that the "One Size Fits All" approach of many marketing and sales books does not work for everyone. That doesn't mean that there are not plenty of good books out there, just that the people who are reading them may not be wired the same way or wired in a way to act on them.

I have said for years to anyone who would listen, that I would rather be home with my family than at any event big or small. Because I am perceived to be a type A personality, most people laugh this off and think that I am kidding them or myself. The reality is that I truly enjoy the simplicity of doing nothing, but of course with the right people in my life. With all that said, once I take on a task or know what I need to do to provide for my family, there is an amazing awakening that comes over my body and mind that allows me to truly excel when at a business or social gathering. I think it comes from my understanding of time and purpose.

> *Here is what I know about me and I try not to take for granted:*

I really enjoy people (I joke that I don't, but they fascinate me on every level)

I really enjoy Conversation (Doesn't matter who you are, just

how you are and how we connect)
I do enjoy learning because that turns into knowing which turns into participating, which makes you viable…

I am a great listener with great retention skills (unless you ask my business partner John as it relates to any technology)

I am a great communicator

I am very excitable

I am hyper, and get distracted easily. SQUIRREL

I do better with multiple balls in the air

These traits have clearly been honed in on and if you compare them with their counterparts you will realize they have come a long way.

I am a great communicator – equals I used to talk too much, was annoying or boisterous and was told to shut up a lot.

I really enjoy people – equals when I was younger I got in trouble a lot, talked to anyone who would listen, and bugged people.

Disclaimer on this book

I am conscious and aware that there are some things in this book that may not work for you.

With that said, hopefully you will find one nugget in this book that leads you to the one relationship that will add great value for you. Hope it helps.

Let us learn about you.

Who can I help or who can help me?

Networking comes in all forms; you never know when the receptionist at your office will become your boss. You never know when you're going to need to re-up, helping others help themselves is the best way to secure assistance for you when you need it. I know firsthand who takes my calls and sometimes don't know why, but I do know that most of my interactions in life, at least in my adult life have been led with the greater good in mind.

Several years after I left my position as President of the first company that I was an owner in, my relationship with my prior employees and independent contractors allowed me to have a relationship with them in a different field and sell some products to them, even though I was still learning my new trade. You never know when you will need that relationship.

Even if you attend a Chamber mixer or lower level networking group almost with a business to consumer feel vs. a business to business feel, your end result may be the same, but asking about input and thoughts on behalf of a third party always seem to create a neutrality that benefits you greater than a direct sales approach. It sounds strange at first, but you know you have a great product or service and you know your commitment level but that may not be what your contact is buying, even looking for or wants to engage about, so the delicate balance of asking for input or if they know anybody you can meet or anybody you can connect them to is a better approach even with boots on the ground.

Plan your strategy and think ahead.

How do you know whether you should play at the low limit table or at the no limit table?

There are different types of players at both, and it also depends on whether you are playing in a charitable tournament, or regular tournament.

Sometimes, if you are not ready to change tables or increase your bet it will not be a good move. For example, if you are in business but you are not sure that either you are going to stay at the company you are with or continue selling the products you have regularly been selling, you need to be aware of the game's outcome if you start an aggressive networking campaign. For the most part, people in general want to see continuity. They want to know that if they directly use you or refer you to one of their clients or friends that you are going to stick with the business for which they referred you. This is why, even when you are known as a person who always gets things accomplished when switching into a new field some people may embrace you and want to help you out with opportunities, but for the most part they will probably not place you in front of their best contact. They will most likely tread lightly as they need to see that you possess the same abilities you once had or you will be just as committed to your new role.

Where this is really common is when you as an employee or a business owner are regularly touting how great your products and services are and those that your company has to offer. Unfortunately, once you decide it is time for you to move on, you or at least most of us, start painting a less than desirable picture of where we were or why we are leaving. So, think about this for a minute. You spent most of your career up until now, selling people on you, your values and where you were and all of a sudden you tell your client all the stuff that has happened behind the curtain.

The fallout from that can be catastrophic; more sophisticated referral sources will assess this information in a way that could be detrimental to your relationship. Imagine sitting at the table playing your cards and you have been aggressively betting and raising all the way through the game, people are scared, but a couple are staying in and all of a sudden you get to the river and you truly have no hand, but you realize you can't go out so you make one more bet, and someone calls you. Now, you have to show your cards for what you really are, in this case you had a plan, but even on its best day it didn't match up to what the other hands on the table could be, so others now know your strategy, they know your tell. You will struggle at that table moving forward. I'm definitely not telling you not to play the game, on the next page are some ideas on how you may play the networking game better.
    1. Remember that a transition to and from another opportunity should be truly about you and your needs.
    2. The less focus on why you decided to leave (because of the

negative undertones) the better.

3. Depending on how you position your exit, if you moved on because of the struggles you had with your private company, people will wonder why you continued to keep them in a place you weren't comfortable with until you were ready to move.

4. If it is a sudden move, you should own it for what it is. People in general are appreciative if they feel you have their best interest in mind.

   a. keep in mind if it's too soon, you may have to be more patient to get the client to understand why you left and have their best interest in mind.

5. If you're just beginning, try to create a balance between your abilities and the reason you are at XYZ Company and what they offer for your client.

a. This is valuable in that it embraces your strengths and your company's strengths without getting you caught in an environment that ultimately may not be right for you down the road.

BEFORE YOU PLAY... KNOW THE RULES

Chapter 2

Am I a Farmer or a Miner?

Farming vs. Mining...

At every level there is more to learn, some people say they are in a networking group, show up to every meeting, tell you how great they are and that is the way it's done. The reality is that nobody is going to walk into a room and say that their office staff are fighting, they struggle to meet goals, they are a one person show eating paycheck to paycheck. That means we need to peel away the layers and find out who we're working with on our own. We need to find out who they are by learning what makes them tick, what's important to them, what is their hot button at that moment.

Focusing on what we are selling rather than what they are buying is one of the biggest problems that sales people and people in general still have. Usually the product or service we offer is something someone already has, so if that is the case they have to leave someone else so we can get the job. Even if we built a better mousetrap and understand they need it, where they are in their process is the focus we need to have.

One of the hardest things for most people to comprehend is the time it takes to truly develop, manage, execute and keep that process and relationship going. One option is to embrace the time it takes and think of yourself as a farmer.

Why a farmer? A farmer will cultivate the land, a farmer will plant the seeds in the cultivated land and that same farmer will figure out how often to water the land. The farmer will patiently watch the growth, manage the growth and prepare for when the product is complete. While it is clearly a lot of waiting, there is also a lot of work preparing and watching the product, hopefully with a good crop at the end of the cycle.

A miner, on the other hand, takes a completely different approach. Probably the best way to describe a miner would be visualizing someone chipping into walls of a mine repeatedly. Constantly chipping, chip, chip, chip into the walls the whole time throwing away what doesn't work and every so often finding something of value. This logic definitely has value and from a business and relationship standpoint there is definitely no shortage of folks who work their way through the world in this fashion. However, it does not have much intrinsic value to me when building a relationship through Networking. Quite frankly, to me it seems like a never-ending use of energy and constantly keeps you having to work harder and harder on each relationship.

How to learn someone's hand?

(How do you learn tells, or if someone is a farmer or a miner?)

If you sell long-term care insurance and estate attorneys are good contacts for you, clearly getting to know one is a goal of yours. The hurdle that most of us overlook is that there are several people who want to get in front of an estate attorney so that attorney may be cautious and guarded about you or too many meetings in general, or they may have a relationship or relationships that are in line so what do you do?

You set out to learn more about them, about their marketing, their strategies as a group, then their niche specifically. You find out their passions, their charities, and their causes. In addition, LinkedIn, Google, Facebook are all viable entry points. It may sound a bit like stalking, but the reality is that if you set out to meet someone in the right networking environment learning as much about them as possible and figuring out how to add value to them is a compliment, it shows your commitment to helping them succeed, accomplish their goals, eat, etc. all with no guarantee to your success. Sometimes it's not that easy and they may not be the right fit for you.

The good news should be that you are that much closer to working with an estate attorney. Think back to when we started this section, you didn't know anything about estate attorneys just that they had the right client for you. Now you know where they go, how they do it, and for the most part how they help a client. You take this info and find another estate attorney and go through the process and see what their needs are and how you can help them. Keep in mind helping them doesn't have to be with a new client, it could be volunteering on their favorite charity, buying raffle tickets for an event, introducing them to your car dealer. Find a new group or association they don't belong to that helps them with life or business. Adding value comes in all forms.

Which Game is right for you?

A key component to networking success or networking gold is to find the network that works for you on all levels, it can't just be business, it can't just be pleasure and it can't just be unscripted. You have to find the rhythm that works for you. You may like to party, you may like to be home, but balance is the key to a truly amazing networking experience.

Which networking group is right for you? This is probably the most difficult part of the Networking process. It is a very personal process; it depends on your unique skills, what you are selling, or what you are ultimately looking to accomplish for yourself. Lastly, it becomes about who you need to meet that may assist you in accomplishing your goals.

Getting a seat at a table is not always the hardest part in business. Finding the right table to sit at is really the key to your Networking success. Most people embrace Networking because they are told that is how to grow their network. Unfortunately, the person leading the charge in getting someone else to network has most likely seen their version of Networking work for them. In many cases they are a product of success that was accidental or the right time and right place, so it may not actually be quantifiable or offer you the tools of creating a long-term networking strategy.

I decided early on in my business career that I didn't want to sell widgets or products that would soon be obsolete. Although I was still in my mid-twenties I also decided I did not want to drive around from customer to customer with a car full of products or samples to sell when I was fifty.

Throughout high school and college I worked in the hospitality industry so I never truly had a sales job or at least so I thought. So getting into sales, specifically as a licensed property and casualty insurance professional was a challenge. Of course I tapped into friends and family right out of the gate, but it took a year and a half to make the same income I made as a valet parking cars at the Disneyland Hotel in Anaheim.

I remember asking one of the insurance producers at my office how he got his business and he said he cold called people, and actually grabbed a phone book and said we have a good apartment building and condominium building insurance program so call property managers. While he stood over me I opened the phone book, with the same excitement that Charley opened his chocolate to find the Golden Ticket in Willy Wonka. I dialed a property manager, got his answering machine and left a message. I sat down and made several more calls all with either a machine or a No Thank You. What a horrible experience, I am never going to make it in sales I thought.

Around the same time, I realized our company was a member of the local Chamber of Commerce as I received a mailer that there was a breakfast meeting coming up. I went to the breakfast. (Which I know is one of the first steps to networking, you have to show up) At that breakfast everyone stood up and introduced him or herself. I met a couple of people at that first meeting, one was a chiropractor and the other was an actuary. They proceeded to tell me about a networking group called Le Tip (see page 75). I had never heard about Le Tip, or the term Networking. It seemed to make sense, you go somewhere, spend some time meeting people and selling your wares and then people give you business. Sounded pretty simple, I could do that. So I joined Le Tip and almost immediately found myself getting referrals for home, auto and renters insurance quotes. I was very excited about this. Soon thereafter I found myself on the board interacting regularly with the other board members with the goal of trying to bring in other people for our group. We had a nice group of people, and it was a good business opportunity but I soon came to realize that we were doing a lot of business together but not truly bringing in business separately. (Point is, the business opportunities seemed to be less about the opportunities and more about giving a referral for the sake of the referral so you didn't have to pay $1.00 for not giving a referral that week) A few months after I found Le Tip another flyer crossed my desk to attend an insurance industry luncheon. My partner at the time did not necessarily understand why I would want to spend time with competitors. I explained to him that it would be a good opportunity for me to learn more about the industry and more about what was happening on behalf of my clients. So I jumped in with both feet and started to understand what the insurance association had to offer. Immediately a member of the board asked me to get involved with a committee and ultimately start the young insurance professionals committee back up in the San Fernando Valley, a suburb of Los Angeles.

After a year of LeTip I started to realize that while I had made some great friends and a few good business connections the time spent wasn't necessarily a good fit for the reward.

WHAT IS THE RIGHT TABLE FOR YOU?

EXERCISE

Play one game with the cards you are dealt and write down the outcome. (Page 128 for more information regarding playing cards)

1. Write 2 sentences about the outcome and include what type of person the cards show you are?

    1.

    2.

How do you as that person adapt to the hand?

Play 5 more games depending on what else you are trying to accomplish.

2. Write 2 sentences on the average outcome and include what type of person the cards show you are?

    1.

    2.

How do you as that person adapt to the hand?

Helpful Hint: - Playing the game several times will make you have to think about the differences with yourself and whether you are a Farmer or a Miner. As you learn the different cards you should also start to learn how to interact and adapt to each situation.

The Cards you are dealt?

IN THE BEGINNING… How it starts – The first two cards dealt are called Hole Cards because they are dealt face down.

The Buy-In

The amount a player spends to get into a game or tournament.

Prior to the BUY IN, you need to figure out a few key things about Networking.

Is it for me? Just like sales isn't for everyone, Networking isn't either. What can make Networking feel more comfortable is that most people network daily and just don't realize that is what they are doing. If you are willing to be patient and in some instances selfless and accept that you may not see a reward on everything you do, then yes Networking is for you. Over the years there have been countless times when I have asked people how I can help them and have helped them without any direct or indirect benefit in return. At the same time there have been several times in my business and professional life that I have relied on others around me to spread my gospel and help me without benefit to themselves and with that help I have accomplished untold gains across the board.

How do you make the cards you are dealt work for you?

Throughout this book the theme remains the same as it relates to helping others before you help yourself. In this chapter, I steer away from that premise with the goal that I can directly assist a group of people who I see as deserving to gain first and foremost. As it relates to veterans, widowed and divorced men and women, I think finding the right network that can help you is a real necessity. It doesn't mean that you won't add value or shouldn't use the same long-term thought process, just that you may have a shorter runway to get where you are going.

Sometimes, even while sitting at a poker table, the other players know when you need a win. They don't necessarily give you their money, but they will fold based on your determination to win the hand. The goal for you is to help other people at the table to want to see you have success so you stay involved for multiple games. In Networking hopefully everyone brings something to the table, and if you find the right table, the other players will realize what you bring for everyone.

Every situation is different, whether you are a veteran, active military, recently widowed or divorced, new or longtime sales person, just trying to meet people; everyone starts with a different set of cards.

In every one of those situations there is an option that works for you. For the purposes of this chapter, let us start with the veterans, divorced and widowed individuals for business purposes.

EXERCISE

What is an elevator pitch and how do you prepare for it?

An elevator pitch should be 30-60 seconds, and about whom you are, what you do, why you are unique and who is your target market.

Answer the questions below:

Who are you?

What you do?

Why are you unique?

Who is your target market?

You should be memorable.

Helpful Hint: As long as you hit the key points above it is ok if your elevator pitch is not as polished as other people around the table.

VETERANS and ACTIVE MILITARY

Whatever your beliefs of politics of why, how or what causes us to send men and women into battle, the one thing that should be clear is that those who serve deserve our respect. How much better can you define a selfless act, than someone fighting and willing to die for people they do not and most likely will never meet? What happens when these amazing men and women return to civilian life or even transition while still active or in the Reserves is where their real struggles can begin.

So why do they need help Networking you may ask? I regularly interact with active military, recently and not so recently released veterans and it is amazing to me just how little understanding these folks have as it relates to using their network or centers of influence. It does make sense, however, when you think about the fact that throughout their duty, being told when, where, how and why to do things is who they become. The expectation of becoming one with the rules, and one with the process does not just go away the moment they are now out and on their own. Additionally, not really understanding your benefits when you leave or how to use them can cause most veterans to move on without knowing.

Even using the GI Bill, which thankfully has become more streamlined and easier for veterans to obtain, but even something as simple as that makes for a difficult task for these young veterans. They served their country, they are now in their early twenties and take advantage of their GI benefits to get into a good college or university and start to work their way through. All the time, they are unsure and in some cases do not know how or are unable to even start up a meaningful conversation with the other students in their classes. Their minds are full of how different they are, how they have nothing in common with these kids who may even be similar in age. Finding the network that is right for a veteran may take some time and several different tables. Younger veterans may not relate to older veterans, married veterans may not relate to single veterans and of course that all works both ways. Spending time trying to find that network is key. Working through the process of who is not right for you, sometimes accomplishes the goal of who and where is right for you. If you are getting out of the service in the near future or have recently got out you should find a handful of places that may be physically desirable (by that, I mean close in proximity to where you are or will be living.) There are so many great programs out there. Colleges and universities in every town seem to have their finger on the pulse of the veteran community. Everyone I have met that works in a school environment seems to know where the various different veterans are. Creating a game plan to find a network will play an integral role in your post military life. Even if it is only for a short time find a network that can start you on the right foot.

READING EXERCISE

How does your personal experience help you in Networking?

An example of this is a Real Estate Agent who recently got divorced and spent time dealing with their issues and are at the same time ready to move forward. People in general who have gone through it have surrounded me. It is an experience that you learn from. You can take that experience, whether you have gotten past it, are in the middle of it, or truly have not had time to deal with it yet. While it clearly is your problem you can rest assured that as much as you think yours is a unique struggle, or you don't know how to get past it, there are others, and a lot of them in the very same boat that you find yourself in.

If your strength is to understand what you have just gone through or are going through, one of the things you can do and should do is figure out how you can help others. Don't focus on getting the sale. If you are a Real Estate Agent focus on understanding the process of going through a divorce and having to deal with all the real estate issues that go along with it. Once you understand the process then you embrace explaining it to as many people as possible. What this accomplishes is empathy, it is truly your willingness to take on a task that people going through your struggle will appreciate. Someone you help may not be ready to have you sell their house or help them buy a house, they may even make you work harder, but knowing that you understand their process will make them that much more comfortable to listen to you and take your feedback as gospel. Whether it is gospel to them or not, it is your knowledge as a buying or selling expert to provide the needed guidance they need to accomplish their goal rather than what may be in your best interest. Be clear that when someone decides you are a good person to go to or refer to, it doesn't always have to be based on your success in getting the sale. It has to be based on your willingness and understanding of the situation and how best you handle it. So back to starting out again in the space you need to be in or embrace. Back in the game, even if you are not an extroverted person and whether your ability is that of an educator, engineer or architect this will be key to your success in the world of Networking. Once you hone in on that trait and figure out how to redirect it for your benefit, you will see the world differently and even if you don't see it, it will still be different.

FOLLOW UP TO EXERCISE ABOVE:

Do you think this Real Estate Agent in the story is a farmer or a miner?

Why do you think so?

Helpful Hint: Think about the Real Estate Agent process. Very patient, understanding of the time it may take, willing and committed regardless of outcome. Now, think of whether that takes a Farmer or a Miner.

As a 19 year old I was the one left holding the bag as they say when my dad died. My mom who to this day is one of the strongest people I have ever met, had to figure out her life after my dad died in a matter of weeks and months. Where to live, how to live and how to give her young adult children what they needed to keep going. Think about that, you build a lifetime and with that, make decisions that will work for you both, and suddenly it is just you, and all that planning goes out the window. What do you do? Where do you turn? Understanding your current network and your need to either expand your network, or your desire to change it altogether is quite common. Knowing how to do it and making it happen is another story. What you tend to find with your current network, is that there may be a lot of great memories and great people with a great desire to support you, but those relationships are not going to be the same. Your network of friends can't help but feel sorry for you, want to treat you differently and use every skill they have not to let you know how they really feel. So you set out on a journey to find the right group that fits your needs. You set out to find an objective third party who wants to help, but isn't necessarily caught up in your emotion. First things first, try everything; do not rule out anything unless you have tried it.

You may find that Networking and support may go hand in hand initially. However, since as I mentioned previously, Networking is calculated and cause driven, you may be able to find the right relationships through Networking more so than a support group.

It really depends on you and how well you move forward. Also, how important and quickly moving forward has to happen. You may have to take on the role of both parents and provide differently than you did before. By nature you may find that grabbing control of everything and everyone else around you, is more important than dealing with your own struggles. In any case, finding a new network of people who embrace what you are looking to accomplish and even though they know where you have been and where you are now as it relates to being widowed, their energy will be focused on what you are trying to accomplish as opposed to the emotional side of your world. Do not take the lack of emotion and focus on your objective as less than genuine or that people in your new Networking circles don't care, most likely it's because they are new to your world and most likely will never be as connected to your world and life before you lost your spouse or partner, which can ultimately help you move forward with your new direction.

What to do when you are recently divorced?

Clearly throughout our lives we all have a pivotal moment where everything seems to collide together. One such collision time is the process of divorce. While I have been married for over 20 years and could never imagine life without my bride, I did have a business partner for several years who happened to be family. When we parted ways, it definitely became about who kept the business contacts, relatives and even some of the friends. So, I offer this fact based feedback with a basic understanding of your frustration, ability to have to figure out the kids' schedules, when to go to certain events, which holiday parties to go to, etc.

While it also may be a liberating time and a time of exploration, now more than ever, understanding how to enhance your network is all too important. However, your emotions positive or negative about your recent life change is so new that your decision making process may not be at the level they already are. Now is one of those times to try sitting at different tables a game at a time. You may have to quickly pick up the pieces, maybe find a new home, new career, new school or environment for your kids. Regardless of the tasks at hand that you face, you may have to find your new network faster than others. As it relates to business, most likely the people who surround you are friends and relatives who have been there to support you and hopefully will remain intact as such. Most likely, however that same group of people may not be able to add the value you need to move forward in new directions when it comes to finding work or starting a new business venture. If you are back in the workforce for the first time in a while, below are a few groups that may help you find what you are looking for.

1. Chamber of Commerce mixers.
2. Religious organization mixers.
3. Men's or Women's business groups.

4. Local Meet ups.

These are good groups due to their diversity in attendance, by that I mean you don't necessarily know why someone is there until you get to know them, but with so many people at these types of events you should be able to find the right person or people to assist you with finding the right direction for you. Once you find your path and are on your way, narrowing down, which group is right for you will become easier.

Chapter 3

How should you bet?

The Ante

A forced bet contributed by all players before cards are dealt as a way to create a pot. Everybody that plays is still on a level playing field; this is the calm before the storm. You have committed to use Networking to move forward, but have not had to commit time, energy, or financial resources until the initial Ante, and in Texas Hold'em once you Ante you may also become the small or big Blind.

How do my cards compare?

Now that you have decided to move forward in a specific Networking direction by committing time, energy and/or financial resources it would be great to know how your cards compare. By this point you should have some idea what the goals of the group are, and what you plan on accomplishing through your involvement. Networking is about helping others first, which in turn can and most likely will benefit you both. It is ok to be new and still trying to find your way around an organization or relationship.

At this point in the game understanding how your cards compare will give you a starting point into Networking. It will show you how much or how little you know or need to know about yourself and others to move through an organization or a relationship. Over the course of a few short interactions you should be able to get to know the other players, get a look at how they play, their tells and then decide if you want to stay for the next round. For most of us truly understanding how our cards compare is hard to do from an objective point of view. We may feel like we shouldn't be there, don't belong or are uncomfortable. On the other hand, we may feel like everyone should want to get to know about us, our hobbies, our business, etc. A good way to figure out what value you bring to the table, and at the same time start to figure out the other players is to reach out to a friend, confidante, fellow employee or a completely neutral third party, like a mentor or consultant.

By having an objective person assist you in understanding your goals, other players and the group as a whole you may learn the best way to work through that specific set of interactions without wasting valuable time. By understanding the cards you are dealt and figuring out how to use them you can decide how to move forward more efficiently. The way most of us tend to waste both our time and financial resources is when we perceive that what we are selling, in this case ourselves, is more important to someone than what they really want or need. In a nutshell, all too often we focus on what we have to offer rather than what someone is looking for. This is usually the case in both Networking and Sales.

Several years back through my Networking relationships on a really high level I set out to grow a new division in my company. I spent a significant amount of time, energy and financial resources to build a team of experts specific to working with Business Managers, based on interactions I had with others who shared with me what that industry was missing.

I was targeting high-level CPA's, commonly known as Business Managers, and through my Network of relationships, I did have their attention, the products they needed, and the right people to service their business. Moreover, I knew they were getting poor service from competitors, and factually they were getting service that was putting their clients in harm's way. Basically, I went all in, playing my own hand, rather than considering what the other players thought of theirs. You may even say I attempted to control the table. Ultimately in the short run I learned an expensive lesson on how Business Managers thought as a community and why they didn't move so quickly.

As far as I was concerned we had everything they needed. The one thing I didn't keep in mind, which should have been Networking 101 for me, was that even though I thought I hit every hot button they had and needed to be filled in reality they didn't think they needed it.

Understanding the way others in the group think and act will ultimately help you figure out how your cards compare as you position yourself within your new organization or relationship. Hopefully, through the process of figuring out others you will figure out how your cards compare. You will move on to the next level because you enjoy it and see a mutually beneficial seat at the table.

In the case of the Business Managers, getting them to transition to my company was only possible when an outside influence, which happened to be the Attorney General of New York accusing several of my competitors of Bid Rigging Insurance Premiums, caused them to move over.

And yes, we did succeed in amazing growth from the Business Managers after that.

Fast forward to the next few years where that division had about 40 employees in it and several thousand policies; it was definitely a networking nightmare!

Some of the daily and weekly tasks others and I performed included:

Walking around and visiting each employee's desk to make sure they had what they needed to make their day work.

Reaching out to the insurance company reps and management regularly.

Making sure each client had a regular point of contact.

While this scenario may seem like a lot of moving parts in some aspects, it did happen and mechanically does fit well with even the most basic components of Networking at most levels.

In my case, keeping the client happy, insurance company happy, employees happy and making sure each one of those doesn't get caught up in the motion of your emotion was always of paramount importance.

Small Blind - The first forced bet in Texas Hold'em poker and other similar poker games. The small blind is generally equal to one-half the minimum bet rounded up to the nearest chip value.

Whether there is intent or not, most people have a financial stake in the game, the minute they start looking at their options, though it should come as no surprise that your stake (or investment) is made up of actual dollars and sweat equity. Just as in Texas Hold'em, you can start with just your ante, and even though you are in the game, being in a small blind position steps up your chances even though it also empties your wallet or your time faster. Keep in mind, while we are discussing the similarities between Texas Hold'em and Networking, our difference is that we need to consider our Human Capital just as importantly as the dollars it costs to establish our name.

Why is it so important to consider human capital? When you first get into a Networking group or Networking environment most likely you either work for someone or someone has told you how great it has been for them. These are 2 key points

1. Someone directs you to attend an event or a meeting, i.e. Boss, counterpart, other manager, etc.
2. You just launched your brand (you) company. And you want to get the name out there; your friend told you it has worked for them.

What most people fail to pay attention to is the ramping up of their business, what they sell, who they want to meet, what are their goals? All of these are key components to whether or not you will have success and use your time wisely. Most likely all the people in number 1 and 2 will not have the same skills, needs or timeframe that you have, so knowing what you have, how you do things and who you are will be key to your success.

How should I play these cards?

It's not whether you win, but rather how you play.

There are so many different variables to Networking. One key concept that gets lost on most salespeople and people in general is that the client is truly incidental to the Networking process. You may say, wait one minute; the client or my employer pays me. I get my commission from that approach. C'mon, Jeff there better be a good explanation for this.

So here we go. Think about the life cycle of a client, prospect or even an employer that might be a large company. A good client stays with you, is committed to you and what you bring to the table for them, but in the world we live in, mergers, buyouts and job attrition are commonplace. If you specialize in working with manufacturers or distributors and your champion (someone you know drinks the You Kool Aid) ends up leaving to go to a different company where does that leave you? Even though they will embrace bringing you into the fold at their next opportunity, the existing company may already have their version of You and you don't know when that relationship will come full circle and in full force again. This doesn't mean you don't continue that relationship, but you and I both know, that one or both of you may head in a different direction if nothing else, just because of your commitment of time.

Now, to the point of why I say incidental, if you were to find a group of people or an industry association that caters to manufacturers and distributors your focus would be better spent on the relationships with the members of that group. There would be a mix of end user clients, prospects, ancillary companies and individuals that also serve the same industry, and yes, some of those folks may be selling what you are selling. By using a similar energy to the one used to obtain clients instead for the purpose of networking, you may actually succeed in creating relationships that will ultimately lead you to that or other clients with a Champion who can introduce you to multiple prospects or opportunities.

The process of securing access to a prospect that may ultimately become a client may or may not take longer through networking; however, the handoff and introduction from someone you have been networking with will most certainly make that introduction more beneficial.

One thing to keep top of mind as it relates to said prospect or client is that you now have an advocate in your corner, but to maintain that status it is key that the client's experience has a much greater meaning. You are now responsible to the client, their experience and the communications they may regularly have with the person who referred you to them.

Yes, it does seem like you may have now created another layer of a possible adverse reaction, but most of us go into business and sales with the belief that our client or customer experience should be nothing short of amazing. This additional layer of relationship only holds us that much more accountable to that process.

What constitutes a strong hand?

Commitment to the process ultimately creates the strongest hand you can have. The reason this is so powerful is that you hold all the chips. You are in complete control of your strategy, thought process, betting and positioning. What you do with those tools and how well everything else aligns will definitely play a factor in the specific hand's strength, but it is your commitment level to showing up, involvement, willingness to roll your sleeves up and stay in the pot for a long game or series of games that will define the strength of your hand. Also, keep in mind, winning transactions will definitely help you grow your business, but figuring out your strategy to be surrounded by the right people at the table will make a transaction less important to your process, and thus as discussed the end user client interaction will become incidental. Don't lose sight of its importance or of your importance to give great customer service and experience, but at the same time as it relates to Networking focus on the multiple opportunities and how you can help enough people to find enough champions to speak you.

Flop

The first three community cards dealt face up on the table.

At this moment you see the flop, assessing what you have and then you are looking around feeling pretty good about your interactions, someone wants to meet for coffee, someone wants your number. Someone may even have a question for after, but remember not to get too excited because the next card could be a game changer.

Networking and sales in general is full of peaks and valleys. You need to figure out what will work for you as it relates to managing your emotions. These would be your tells. Too eager, too upset, unsure, you get the picture.

EXERCISE

Do you know what your Tells are?

1. What 3 positive tells do you believe you have?
2. What 3 negative tells do you believe you have?
3. What do you think you could do differently to avoid the nega   tive tells?
4. How can you focus and use your positive tells to grow your network?

The Turn

Sometimes when you think you are at a pivotal point in a conversation or trying to understand how you can add value or gain value, bam.... the turn happens... Someone jumps in, or the person you are talking to gets sidetracked. What do you do now? Don't try and finish what you're saying or continue on your mission, you need to adapt, you need to focus, you need to grab decorum and adjust. This is such a common occurrence in Networking groups; I have seen it get squirrelly really fast. I have been on the side I am telling you to avoid; I have continued with my discussion, I have continued to finish my story. It doesn't add value, it doesn't get the point across, what it does do is leave a memory with the person you are trying to make an impression with and it just may be the impression you weren't planning on. So change it up. How do you prepare for it?

The Follow Up

The follow-up is a very important piece in the Networking process. You can pick up cards, shake hands and say hello, send an email to look for an opportunity but the follow-up is a key component to Networking. If you get a referral you follow up with the person that gave it to you follow up with the person they referred to you and then go back to the person who gave it to you and tell them how it went or went or where you stand. You continuously do this through the process of that referral. Understanding how the person who is referring you expects to remain involved makes it easier for you to know how they would like you to handle it. For instance the trusted advisor, coach, financial advisor (or a wealth manager in some cases) and different types of attorneys like to be kept in the loop and like to be able to have that conversation about the client to see how the process is going.

EXERCISE

How do you follow up on a referral?

1. Reach out to the person you were referred to.
2. Reach back to the person who gave you a referral with an up date of what you have done and where you stand with the referral.
3. Make sure you continue open communication with both the person you were referred to, and whom you received the referral from
4. If the referral source is an Attorney, CPA, Financial or Wealth Advisor traditionally they like to remain in contact with you throughout the process.

Helpful Hint: Your interactions with #4 should accelerate the relationship you are working on, and regular communication on behalf of their client or friend is one of the best ways to add value to them. In addition, you should use this time to understand how those same professionals fare with their clients so you can in turn seek out and find them opportunities that may help their businesses grow.

Avoid overplaying your hand

Sometimes, when we are so engulfed in conversations and interactions at networking events, we may get caught up in the excitement of this new or ongoing relationship that we ultimately can damage it before we get to the next level. I remember in one specific instance I had a fairly strong relationship with a Real Estate Agent, we talked about family, friends, etc. And over several interactions we developed a friendship with a great business component. It was that same fast relationship that afforded us the opportunity to joke with each other and really feel good about it. I introduced another person into the mix and immediately they saw how we played off each other and jumped right in. All was good until the new introduction pushed the envelope because he didn't know his audience, boundaries and limitations. It was quite a shame, because I truly saw an opportunity for them to work together, but since all the layers hadn't been peeled and these two truly never had a chance to take it to the next level, they went from what I thought would be a great Reciprocal relationship to a missed opportunity on both sides.

Is this the right hand for me?

Sometimes, even what appears to be the best relationship opportunity may not be what it seems. Knowing what the right hand for you is key to your success. I remember when an Insurance company I had represented specifically for my High Net Worth and Entertainment clients with wanted me to meet a very high level Life insurance guy, before I met with him I asked around to find out what he was like. Interestingly I got a similar response from everyone I asked, they all said he knows everybody. Beyond that I couldn't get anything else. It got me thinking, what is it about this guy that I can't get a he's a good guy or he's a bad guy, just that he knows everybody. So, because someone went out of his way to connect us, I obliged. It was a very interesting interaction. He invited me to be his guest at a baseball game, I left my car in a parking lot and he picked me up with a younger associate closer to my age. Immediately there was this banter between them, name-dropping and talking about whom they worked with and how I could have access to those clients as well. We even got into a discussion of how they shared revenues of these clients. Anyway, I kept moving forward, we get to the game and yes true to the statements I heard, this guy knew everyone and made sure I knew he knew everyone. So much so that that the new owner of the team was introduced to me and even later that same night the team's owner yelled across the room over a bunch of people and said something to me, to the effect, "see Jeff, told you they were great seats." I was all of 30 something and for anyone else that would have been an amazing interaction and story and I know there were definitely more to be had, but I just couldn't get past how he knows everybody. Other than an obligatory follow up lunch, I just decided we should part ways and move on, nothing bad, nothing good. I just felt he was not the right person to share connection opportunities with.

The interaction above for me, probably best describes a time before the turn, you will really need to figure out the right time and place for you to move forward or move on. Before the turn, seems to be a good time while you are actively looking for the right groups, organizations and causes to get involved with, but early during this time you should either stay on course and committed or move on. Once you get past the turn your expense will increase and of course the possibility of the reward should increase, but you can no longer just stroll through the groups without commitment.

How will you know when to move on to a different group? When you realize that you aren't committed or do not find yourself interested in what's going on in a group that is a good sign. What you need to watch out for is that you don't want to feel like the group is beneath you or not where you are, because that is a tough place to move on from. It is better for you to realize that you are not able to focus at that level. It may sounds like semantics, but the hardest thing you can do is go back into a group that you left because you felt you were better than it.

You are the New Business Card?

Not too long ago, business cards were a status symbol, a way to say look at me, who I am, my company, my title and just by looking at it the person you gave it to instantly felt they new who you were. Most importantly the person you gave your card to gained a perception of your status within the organization. If your card said you were a Vice President that meant something.

Recently, maybe 15 years ago or so, (and yes that is fairly recent in the world, not just my world) people would embrace titles for their cards that didn't have the same meaning; they were actually calling themselves Vice President. At one point in my old insurance agency, I think there were over 15 people walking around with the Vice President title, while there were only 4 officers of the company. I didn't take issue with it, nor do I take issue with it, but what I do need to point out is I believe this was the start of a new era.

This was the start of a time when it became more prevalent for people to engage more, learn more about who they were dealing with. At the same time as the internet really started to pick up steam and you could learn more about a person, who they are and what they have accomplished, you can also learn if their card matches their person. In a sense, you have become your new business card. A key component as to why this is so important is because at this moment in time the things you can learn about someone you are trying to enter a relationship in at whatever level are amazing. You need to be conscious of you, your story and your commitment. That is what makes your first interaction so important. You have to understand that from the minute you say, who and what you are or are trying to be has to pass the online gaming test. Even if you haven't embraced a true online gaming mentality you have to assume that the person or group you want to connect with will do some serious research on you, your story and your business and social world. In the same discussion you need to learn the basic tools about the online Gaming world yourself, because remember two can play at that game.

Too much or not enough?

Success is a double edge sword, in order to make partner in a law firm or CPA firm you need to bring in clients, but you also receive pressure from existing partners to work on the harder clients and cases. This push and pull tends to make it harder to get out there and bring in more clients and become the rainmaker you may or may not be capable of achieving. At the same time, future rainmaker or not, you will definitely be expected to bring in your own clients to become a true partner.

Learning how to throttle in with networking while creating an increasing income stream is key to your ultimate success.

While it does not happen rapidly or even steadily in some cases, it happens nonetheless. It's all about temperament and timing. It's like learning to drive a stick shift car. While most young people today will never have that experience the best way to describe it is to put one foot on the clutch and one foot on the gas and ever so gently push the gas down while releasing the clutch. Ultimately they should both meet in the middle and you're off, but a rocky start is nothing to pull back on.

Chapter 4

The Turn

Why am I here?

Networking separates functional ROI (Return on Investment) from indirect ROI; you need to believe in the numbers, it truly is a numbers at bat concept, just as in baseball.

A seat at the Table

I have discussed the various groups I am or have been involved with. The one group that has remained constant throughout my business life is called Provisors, which back when I started was known as Professionals Network Group (PNG). Keep in mind, most people had not heard of the term network or networking as it is used throughout this book, it definitely wasn't well understood and used in terms of connecting or creating relationships as it relates to Networking. Networking was almost looked upon poorly and frowned upon, as most people didn't understand its purpose.

When I had the opportunity to attend my first PNG meeting it came after I had gone through a very detailed phone interview process, and once I got past that I was invited as a guest to my first networking meeting. It was amazing, I had been a part of so many groups, up until this point and met so many great people. This meeting somehow seemed different; it seemed to be a seat at a different table, a higher-level table. The introductions were better, the caliber of business professionals was higher. Lastly, I noticed I was definitely the youngest and probably least experienced person in the room.

The one thing that I took away from my phone interview before the meeting was that PNG was about helping others first. So, armed with a blank yellow pad of paper and a zest for helping others that I learned from my days working at the Disneyland Hotel I was ready for my seat at the table. Immediately, members started in with their elevator pitches and industry updates. Next on the agenda, was this item called Needs, Deals and Wants. This was it, the start of my entrée into helping others. One after another, members would state what they were looking for, one guy was writing a book and looking to get introductions to certain people. Another person wanted to meet the head of a specific company. Next came an executive recruiter looking to hire an outside CFO for a company. I struck gold; writing down everyone's needs paying attention to the very end. I had my marching orders. I knew this was my way in. This was easy, helping others is who I am, how perfect was this? So I left this meeting and immediately went back to my office and reached out to my few resources in hopes they could help me connect some of these people and their needs. Through every resource I had ultimately I was able to fill a couple of the Needs requests from that meeting. While completing the task was not that simple, it was those simple referrals that started me down the road to becoming a connector. I established relationships with several people from that first day, which have remained and continue to be mutually beneficial relationships.

How will you know when to move on to a different networking group?

1. Are you not committed or not engaged?
2. Are you not interested?
3. Do you regularly start to miss meetings and events?
4. When you start to feel you are better than the group, and feel you have nothing more to gain, what do you do?

Helpful Hint: It is better to confront the fact that the group is not for you, rather than make it linger. If people start to see you are not committed, stop showing up or seem like you are better than the group that is the impression you will leave on them. A straight forward approach to leaving will keep relationships intact.

So how did my giving come back around in PNG? About six months after I joined PNG showing up at the table, helping others and being in the right place and right time, I received the referral that would ultimately allow me to create a continual income stream over the next fifteen years.

In the early days of my PNG experience, I was embraced by a

financial advisor who viewed me as good candidate to cross-refer business to. Rather quickly he and I shared a couple of referrals to each other. As I mentioned, about six months into our relationship, the financial advisor reached out to me and told me that a Fitness Association was looking for a new insurance agent. I thanked him for the referral and reached back to the client's business consultant. Once I met with them I realized this was not about the association procuring insurance, but rather looking for a partner who could truly assist their customers with their insurance needs. At the time, it was a very small industry with a Wild West type of attitude. From day one, meeting one it was clear that the association, which is called the Aerobics and Fitness Association of America (AFAA) which had about 250,000 members had set itself apart from the rest through the leadership of its owner Linda. It was Linda's goal to have us create a best in class process and series of insurance products for her membership base. After months of wrangling and negotiations on how we were to partner together to offer these amazing products, we got the order.

I was told by the consultant who brought Linda and I together, "Now, comes the hard part, be careful what you wish for." He couldn't have been more right. So now, I landed this great opportunity to provide products to 250,000 people. I had to take credit cards…. (Unheard of in insurance) I had to have an (800) number…again unheard of, and oh by the way, my premiums for the policies started at $131 per year… again, unheard of. Oh, and by the way, we had to pay for the printing and marketing pieces that would reach these 250,000 members.

EXERCISE

Take out a yellow legal pad (or your favorite pad) and your favorite pen.

Needs and Deals to write down:

1. Who do you need to help?
2. Who can help you?
3. Who should you reach out to that always needs something?
4. What is the perfect referral for you?

No turning back

Managing relationships within the client's network.

Through the process of getting the order to move forward, I realized that this was also ultimately a client. There were so many people involved in different areas of AFAA that this needed to be treated like one big Networking opportunity. What I had to do next, and was conscious of at the time is that the people at AFAA were already busy and already bogged down with their own work, and now they have been tasked to work with me, which in itself was an additional layer to add to their already busy lives.

First things first, I took great advantage of AFAA's all access offer for me to learn and meet with their people. Whether, it was their magazine, marketing, mail campaigns, instructors, writers, reception desk, it didn't matter, I needed to understand their operation and the people who supported it. Over the next several months and into the next several years I forged deep, truly meaningful relationships with several key people. I attended their trade shows, worked at their booth, organized the booths, and understood their products, services and concept almost as much as I did my own products that I offered through them.

In the early years, I became a boots on the ground go to guy for Linda in sharing my overview of the industry, the events, and of the traffic that came through. I became so embedded in AFAA, their business and the fitness industry in general, that I successfully picked up other clients, and relationships that have held strong to this day.

What did I do right with AFAA?

I learned their business.
I learned their needs and hot buttons.
I learned about the people, the employees, the contractors, vendors, etc.
I was 100% committed to their success.
I embraced the time as my own.
I adapted my networking skills to each individual.

Reading the other players at the table.

How did I manage to become part of the AFAA team?

1. I understood who the players were at AFAA and their roles.
2. Learned what Linda and her people were doing.
3. Looked for opportunities to add value.
4. Remained an active objective participant in their business.

In doing so, I genuinely became a part of the AFAA team and added value at every step, by attending trade shows with them, working their booth, learning more about their competitors and immersed myself in understanding what they did so I could help them grow at any chance I had.

Turn

The fourth community card dealt faces up in a Texas Hold'em game.

Passive

Adjective to describe a player who frequently calls and rarely bets. Networking is all about betting on yourself, you can't wait until someone decides it's your turn to play

Sandbagging or (call or check)

Holding back and calling despite the fact that you have a very good hand, usually to disguise strength, provoke bluffs, and to check-raise.

When my first business was firing on all cylinders it was hard not to get jaded and caught up in the mechanics of its everyday needs, there were definitely points and times where others would express our differences and while I downplayed them, clearly there was an underlying energy that could not be stifled. At least by remaining grounded and not going all in I maintained a level of relationships with almost everyone from my receptionist to the CEO's of a major insurance companies. Both sides need to know who you truly are and how you will respond regardless of the outcome.

(The day we got T4 the last Terminator movie, and the day we lost it)

One of the biggest tests of networking for me while President of the insurance agency, was the day that we lost the production insurance package for the movie, which at the time was code named T4, which later became Terminator Salvation. One of my sales people had a great relationship with key players at the production company and had a great relationship with the person who ran the insurance company we placed it with. Needless to say, somebody at the production above our contacts made a decision to change insurance agents. At the same time, the insurance company representative stated to us in no uncertain terms they would not cancel and rewrite the policy, thus allowing us to still get paid. Clearly it did not work out that way and the insurance company did cancel and rewrite the policy.

So what was I to do, a dedicated sales person who worked for me for quite some time and an insurance company we did a lot of business with and a client who clearly made their decision to move on. It was heartbreaking; we deserved the account, we earned the account and all of a sudden, we lost it. The networking side of me knew what a struggle the insurance company person went through and that I needed to support his decision, as we needed to keep the channels open. At the same time, I cherished and still do to this day the relationship I had and have with this sales person, so we had to sit down and go through the motions to fight for him, but set the expectations that the battle was only as good as his contact could make it. Tough work and definitely changed the dynamics across the board, but being able to understand the bigger picture in a situation like that definitely made both those relationships stronger.

Slow Play

While some people in Networking tend to maintain a completely passive strategy almost to the point where they either genuinely or strategically don't want to come off as being there just to get business, in some cases if you really feel good about the value you are adding and see an opportunity to truly become a respected advisor or friend to your new connections, a slow play approach can be a better play and may actually create a stronger hand.

Where the Slow Play approach differs from a Passive approach is that you let people know you are there. You are in the game, you are committed to the cause, you are engaged or engaging and you spend time to decide what your involvement will be. The passive person will most likely call, but rarely bet. While there are arguments on both sides of this in poker, in Networking you have to be involved.

Probably the best way to compare being Passive with Slow Playing your hand if you are still moving forward is as follows:

If you are passive, you wait until someone bets and you match his or her bet.

If you are slow playing you could bet the minimum, which shows people you are still engaged, but it also lets you see who the other real players on the table are that may be good for you.

The way this relates to Networking is that you want to be noticed; you want to say hey I have a seat at the table, and I am using it.

Several years back I wanted to get connected with a guy I met at one of my networking meetings, his passion was this group called the Water Buffalo club. He told me they were a charity set up for the sole purpose of giving back to different charitable causes. It was and is made up of mostly high level lawyers, CPA's and other white-collar professionals. Of all things, they were having a friendly poker tournament with a $50 entry fee. So I thought about it, I like poker, it's a pretty reasonable price point, he is big on his charitable endeavors, and I want to connect with this guy. I got involved in the event, truly enjoyed myself, he and I connected, and it was the start of an amazing friendship and business relationship that literally lasted into his retirement this past year. I slow played my hand by deciding how much to go in, and at the same time I engaged on his level when it was time. Had I remained passive and waited until our next networking event or meeting I don't believe I would have had this great long relationship.

INCLUSION ~ A KEY TO NETWORKS

Why did the Water Buffalo club work for me?

1. I wanted to connect with a specific person.
2. I liked what the group was about.
3. I enjoyed poker.
4. It was a low price point of entry.
5. It was the right table for me.

Helpful Hint: You will find that people with common likes, needs, hobbies, and causes seem to work together easier. Finding these same people who are focused on what you are trying to accomplish still may be a process but it's an easier one once you know have a clear roadmap of who you are.

EXERCISE

What are your hot buttons or what excites you?

1. What hobbies do you have?
2. What type of events do you like to go to?
3. What is your average budget to get one on one with someone?
4. What type of people do you usually surround yourself with?
5. What is your favorite charity or charitable cause?

Is anyone dropping out?

One thing most books in general can't prepare you for is your reaction to other people seated at your table who do the same thing. Let me try and address others in your industry or with the same goals, but keep in mind that by nature we all tend to defend our territory, we all think that the introduction we just made is ours. It is who we are, and of course, let us not forget that feeling we get when somebody succeeds to make headway with a relationship instead of us.

What about when you know your product, service and that your team can do it just as well if not better, and all of a sudden you have to figure out how you're going to react and interact when someone gets in your way.

In my world of Residential Lending and Real Estate, I may go to a Brokers Open House and notice other lenders there, several have been there and usually one is hovering around the agent so you can not get any quality time with them. Being able to assess and adapt to the situation you are most likely walking into, it makes perfect sense to prepare for it. I am not saying to look at their Facebook wall and see what hobbies they are into; I am saying that you need to appreciate the irony that everyone around you has a different approach to accomplishing the same goal. In my case of doing residential loans for people purchasing a home I knowingly and willingly accept that half or more of the people I see on any given day in any open house or real estate networking meeting will be competitors. If this is an integral part of your business you need to accept the fact that people won't get out of the game, but you also need to prepare yourself and hopefully use some of the things you are learning in this book, or at least keep them in mind. The longer you stay, show up and add value; eventually the room will get emptier and emptier of your competitors. (Unless they too are reading this book). The reason is simple…Instant Gratification, we are a society of instant gratification and even though the fast paced world of quick talking sales people has been around for a long time, it wasn't who we were as a people. It is who we are as a people, but if you value the handshake and value commitment, you will succeed in the networking space and remain a viable staple in whatever industry you are in.

Find a Champion.

What is a Champion and how do you find one? In examples like mine within the real estate community where you are running around with several people in your space, look for someone who you see as a Champion in the space. You have to open your mind to the fact that they may not be and in fact probably will not be able to directly help your business, but if they see you as someone who adds value to their energy or themselves in general just letting you hang out at their table makes you one of the cool kids to them. You still have to do the work, but you will find them. They come from all walks of life, they are people with something about them and you just want to be with them. Maybe you are that person, maybe not, but finding that person will be key to your future success.

EXERCISE

Think about and compare a direct sales experience with an indirect sales experience through Networking.

Direct Sales

List some reasons why the sale may not happen.

When a key person or contact leaves the company you are selling to or trying to sell to what happens?

Give an example of when someone will not refer you to others because they don't want you working with competitors.
If a client sells their company what do you think may happen to you and your product or service?

Indirect Sales Experience Through Networking

How do you create a couple of key relationships that can bring multiple clients?

How do you obtain a larger pool of prospects?

What do you think a Champion in networking is?

How does a Champion help explain why you are best person for the job?

Helpful Hint: A champion is someone who speaks well of you and tells others what you do, how you do it, and why they should use you. They are basically a big cheerleader of you. What makes a Champion in networking so important is that their allegiance to you is not dependent on the sale, rather on what you need them to do and who you need them to speak with on your behalf.

Chapter 5

Should we split the pot?

River

The fifth and last community card dealt face up in a Texas Hold'em game.

Pay Off

To call a bet when the bettor is representing a hand that you can't beat, but the pot is sufficiently large to justify a call anyway. There are times when you know you are out of your league and you shouldn't have a seat at the table; nonetheless, win the hand.

What a game changer

A business manager changed my game. I already knew I had hit the big time in business when I started working with business managers. (Business Managers are CPA's and personal managers to Entertainment and High Net worth individuals and their families) I didn't know how much further I could get. Until the two conversations I had with a certain business manager, who is an amazing man who has spent his professional life as a CPA to manage Entertainment and High Net Worth clients throughout their daily lives.

Becoming the business management firm's go to guy in itself was amazing, but the two conversations that resonate with me to this day, went as follows.

One of my top business managers had asked me to find out some information for a client. I told him I would get back to him.

He then said, "When?" I immediately replied, "Tomorrow."

Without missing a beat, he asked, "What time?"

After being thrown off and adjusting I said, "Ten a.m."

I made my calls, got my answers and was prepared to respond to the business manager the next day.

The next morning, I was on a different call, which carried through the 10:00 a.m. time period. It was now about 10:05 and I saw the call come through from the business manager. I continued with my call, and what happened next truly changed my life.

I then saw a call from a consultant to the business manager who I regularly worked closely with, at the same time I received an email from one of my employees that the business manager was on the phone and looking for me. As soon as I got off the phone I called the consultant and she told me the business manager was looking for me and wanted to make sure I was ok, because I hadn't gotten back to him when I said I would. He was used to me following through and up until now I had never let him down. You get the point, from that day on, I learned how, when and why we say what we say and when we say it, we do it. Without a doubt that simple series of interactions over those two days elevated me to another level of table play.

The strategies of the game.

While I am playing cards I often joke to people around me that I don't really pay attention to everyone else's hands in the game. Even though in actuality I do tend to pay attention to my opponents, I am usually focused on how they play rather than what they may have. People are creatures of habit, no matter how hard they try, no matter how many times they change it up, once you understand who they are, you will know what works for you. That doesn't mean you will become their go to person, and it doesn't mean you will always be compatible, but it does mean you will know where you stand after a certain point.

Several years after I stopped working for gratuities in the service business, I was sitting at my desk in my office and it hit me, I really get it, I understand people. What makes them tick, what they need, how they need it, and when they need it.

It was right there all these years and I was doing it, I just didn't know what it was.

It was the ability to make a person's experience the best it could be. Specifically in my case, I really honed in on it through my years working at the Disneyland Hotel in Anaheim. Yes, the original hotel where it all started next to Disneyland. I remember bugging the manager in charge of the bell staff for months trying to get a job with the bell staff. Finally he relented and offered me a job as a page (basically an errand runner). I fought hard and said No, I wanted to be with the bell staff, but I either wanted to be a bellman or a valet. At the same time I had been offered a job at the Ritz Carlton in Laguna Niguel as a valet, the Disneyland Hotel bell staff manager called me to finally offer me the valet position. I remember, at the time thinking I would make more money at the Ritz, but to work at Disney, what an opportunity for a kid from Phoenix.

I took the job, and what followed over the next several years included some truly defining moments. There were so many interactions with so many amazing and interesting people. The one key concept that stuck with me is what kind of experience do you want for the people around you? It should be so simple, but does seem to get lost regularly with people in every walk of life. Don't get me wrong; it would be hard to imagine that you could struggle creating an amazing experience for people in the Disneyland environment. When reality sets in and you realize that not everyone is there to provide a great experience several people are there because they need a job and the pay is good. Not to mention, that being a valet vs. working the Jungle Cruise (which I would have loved by the way) brought in more of the latter. I saw people with their hands out for tips, throwing change down when the tip wasn't big enough, throwing away the keys of people they helped and didn't get tipped from, and of course all the change that went missing from ashtrays (yes, people used to have lighters and ashtrays in their cars) in cars that were parked. I would be remiss if I didn't acknowledge the stick of gum I ended up with from someone's car either.

So now that you know what it was like to be a valet at the Disneyland Hotel, we can get back to the task at hand.

Why do you want to focus so much on someone else's experience? I remember seeing a family standing by the valet stand waiting for another valet to bring up their car. I walked over and asked them how their stay was, where they were going, if they needed any help. The guy mentioned he had not been there since he was a kid, which was easily 25 years earlier, but he had fond memories of this great place like a diner by the park. I immediately thought of a place called Belisles, which was on Harbor about a mile from the Park. He thought that might be it, smiled and went to give me the dollar in his hand. I told him no thanks and that he should give it to the valet, I was happy to help. He left and went on his way. A couple hours later he and his family returned. As soon as he pulled up and got out, he couldn't tell me fast enough how that was the same place he remembered, and he couldn't thank me enough for giving him the feeling of that experience one more time. He gave me $5 to park his car.

So, let's think about that, one dollar to the valet for running to one of the parking areas, getting the car, bringing it back and sending the guest on his way. Now, five dollars for recommending a place I had sent hundreds of people to before him and writing a ticket to park his car. Makes simple sense that he expected his car to be pulled up, but didn't expect to relive an amazing memory, just like the MasterCard commercial…Priceless.

Getting five dollars to give a valet ticket and park a car in itself was more than enough, but what happened next was nothing less than amazing. The night before when my guest returned the car, I noticed he was wearing one of those satin style jackets that people had for sports teams, but his was from a little casino in downtown Las Vegas, one of those shady places most of us didn't tend to frequent back then. Usually they were locals only hangouts. Back to the morning, when he came out with his family, I mentioned that I was off to Vegas after my shift (obviously remembering the jacket, and the car license plate). My guest asked me where I was staying and as any other good college student I said we didn't have a place yet. He then asked me if I had a house phone with an outside line, I obliged, once he had an outside line, he said something to the effect of "Hey, this is _____, do we have any rooms at the Excalibur". He looked over and said, "Jeff, how many of you are going?" He got off the phone and said it's under your name and said if you have any problems let me know. He gave me his card, which said he was the CFO of Circus Circus Enterprises.

I thanked him and he went on his way.

Even as a college kid, I knew not to let him get away. I thanked him from a casino house phone the next day at his office. In addition to that call, over the next couple years we stayed in regular contact as I genuinely knew that I added value to his life, and he saved a poor college kid a room charge for a couple of nights.

How do you bet when different cards come up?
(Page 128 for more information regarding playing cards)

1. Play 5 hands either with someone else or placing two cards away and deal yourself two.
2. Deal the cards through the 7th card.
3. How many games did you win or lose?
4. What did you learn about the hands?
5. Keep practicing to build up strategies.

How do I decide the best use of my time?

For me, the way I make my networking decisions is a process.

For instance if I commit my time to be at a meeting from 7:30 to 9:30 in the morning, why wouldn't I want to make the most of that time. Once I use that time, I don't get it back. If I don't use it wisely I have to take two more hours of my time to try and make up for it. So logically, I should use it wisely the first time. Now let's think about this time. It's a networking event. In this case it happens first thing in the morning, when most of the business world is just picking up steam. Hopefully, the other people showing up are truly there to grow their business or find resources they can use to assist their clients. So we are all on the same page, everybody has a common goal, just showing up without a clear, concise goal of using that two hours wisely does not make sense. Clearly in most cases, this is not a social mixer, we are not out for drinks, and while you may get a chance to learn about someone's business and personal thought process, chances are you will have to have another interaction to start to drill down or peel away the layers. There are many ways to narrow down who you want to meet with. Try not to limit it to "these are the type of people your industry usually gets business from". Simply put, they know that, they expect that and quite frankly if they are good at what they do, most likely they already have a relationship with somebody that is good at what you do. And if so, there are two things that are true, one is that if they are that quick to move on to you, then they will be that quick to move on from you. And two, in most cases I have found someone eager to do business with me without peeling any layers or having any feedback from someone else about me is usually too good to be true. Anyway, you may learn more about a person at this type of meeting than you think. You will learn if they have time for you, you will learn if they want to make time for you, and you will most likely learn if they are looking to learn about you or just tell you about themselves.

All about you.

What are your strengths?
1.
2.
3.
4.
What are your weaknesses?
1.
2.
3.
4.

What are your Hobbies?
1.
2.
3.
4.

What type of events do you like to go to?
1.
2.
3.
4.

What are the different types of people you usually surround yourself with?
1.
2.
3.
4.

What are some charities or charitable causes you like being involved in?

1.

2.

3.

4.

Helpful Hint: Once you figure out the previous page, look for commonalities that may assist you in finding a group to join, people to meet, or a charitable cause to embrace.

I am still here, Now What?

One of the hardest things to really put into your thought process is the time it truly takes to develop, manage, execute and follow through to keep a relationship going. It is imperative that you embrace your time, the human capital you expend and think of yourself as a farmer.

As I previously mentioned, a farmer will cultivate the land, plant the seeds and figure out how often to water the land. The farmer will patiently watch the growth, manage the growth and prepare for when the product is complete and have to remain calm and patient throughout.

Another key concept to Networking success or networking gold is to find the network that works for you on all levels. It can't just be business, it can't just be pleasure and it can't just be unscripted. You have to find a rhythm that works for you. You may like to party, you may like to be home, but the balance is key to a truly amazing networking experience.

Why should you stay in the game, but not the hand?

Just using pure mathematical numbers would consider me a middle aged guy who's has had my share of successes, failures and chaos. By other standards I am a young man in sales and still have a long way to go to be considered old and seasoned. Back in 2008, I decided to leave the company that I was President for and sold all my shares. People thought I was crazy for doing this and I took a lot of grief for it. However, I had a goal and commitment to more family time and less business. That's because by all standards what I was part of and how we built it was stupendous and we were definitely viewed by competitors, clients and others to be at the top of our game. A couple of things important to that transition were that I signed a non-compete for three years not to go after any clients or employees. It was a pretty fair buyout agreement for both sides, by that I mean that we both probably felt shorted yet we both got to move on. My partner got to keep the business for him and his son and I kept my immediate family and my sanity intact.

Because of the emotional nature of my separation with my old partners, I made a conscious decision about the great contacts, friends and business relationships I had built up over the prior 14 years. I did not want my partners to hear or see anything that would make them not want to honor our buyout agreement.

In fact if truth be told, I really never thought I would have anything to do with any of my old clients as they were unique to what I did, but not an integral part of my business life even after the non-compete would be up.

You could say that I tried to make sure employees were in a good place and the public knew it was about me leaving to separate family from business, not any concerns about the company, (and yes, if you like this book, the next one will really get you, my old partner is a relative).

So, when I left the company and relocated my family about a hundred miles south, I shut down my Rolodex (what you may call a database) and decided to simplify everything. What I did know however was that you never know when you will need your network or what you need it for, so even with very little business purpose I continued to attend Provisors meetings, which happened to keep me connected to my network.

After my sale, Networking became about mentoring and not losing the connections and keeping a network because you never know.

I was right. You don't know, ultimately what I thought was me riding off into the sunset, was me riding into the fog, needing to do business in an environment I never really worked in, in a business that I didn't have any experience in. Now of course as a guy who grew a company from 15 people to 80 people I know people and know how to build a business model that makes sense, so I partnered with my good friend John Soricelli.

Why did I keep a seat at the table?

In the late 1990s, I met an outspoken, larger-than-life guy on the elevator in my old office building. On that short ride, we realized both of us were in PNG and now had offices on the same floor. About five years later, we were now both moving to new locations in Woodland Hills. We had lunch and showed each other our new offices. My friend had been out of PNG for a few years, feeling that he was too busy. But at this lunch, he said he was going back, because he wanted to help with the growth of (now) ProVisors. I thought this was great, but I also didn't know how people would respond to someone coming back when they left because they didn't need it anymore. Unfortunately a couple weeks later my friend passed away, but it was that friendship and that specific interaction that kept me in ProVisors, even when, a few years later, I didn't have anything to sell.

So I kept Networking, although it was more like Networking to mentoring to Networking with no purpose and whether it was unfounded or not I felt I was not adding enough value to people that were specifically getting together for business purposes.

I felt great in social Networking situations, but when it came to business to business Networking and even connecting I didn't find myself up on current events, not up on my industry or anyone's industry for that matter. I was like a car not working on all cylinders.

As I mention throughout the book, hopefully, you will find that one nugget and it adds value to you at any different level, business, pleasure, charity, etc. Even in fast paced business sales fields such as life insurance, stock and mutual fund brokers, lead based, MLM's and forced referral based industries, long term networking strategies can be key to continuous success. While Networking in the traditional sense may not work well when you get into that fast paced sales mode, it is definitely worth acknowledging and addressing at some level since you may be unsure if the fast paced business model is right for you. Building a network that can assist you whether or not you stay in that field or make a transition to a new job or even a new type of industry will help you in the long run.

Chapter 6

ONLINE POKER

Social Media

If you haven't already reached this in your business or personal life, you get to a point where you are looking for that amazing contact or your big opportunity. In baseball you may consider it as hitting a triple or a home run. In Texas Hold'em, you would consider a Straight Flush or Four of a Kind to be triple to home run stature.

So, unless in business your last Four of a Kind took you out of the game and you are living on a beach somewhere with not a care in the world, you need to think of your win as just one of many that need to happen throughout your game of life. There are so many games you still have yet to play.

You may never give up your seat at the table, and as discussed in several areas throughout this book, you need to play multiple games simultaneously.

I have been fortunate over the years to have a few Four of a Kinds and they have not only changed my life, but have also carried me to the next opportunity, that is where we now take the time to take our game online.

As much as we discuss Networking, the handshake and the inter-action, in this day and age it is very hard to ignore the locally global reach the online world of social networking affords us. This would be the virtual handshake, and understanding how valuable and important the online world is to the complete success of your business or Net-working in general.

How you communicate.

How you throw out your intentions isn't just there for your intended audience.

It becomes a permanent piece of history.

The minute you post something to a forum, group, your Facebook, LinkedIn, Twitter, etc., you've created a non-retractable bit of information. Yes, you can take back what you say, yes you can alter your communication, but what you said is there for the taking.

As large as this world is, you will find that depending on the purpose for your post and where you share it, most likely within a few short degrees of someone you know will see your words.

There are two sides they can come from, either:

A. Great info, thanks for sharing, I am going to send this around
B. Can you believe so and so said this?
You have to keep in mind, never before has the statement,
"For every action, there is an equal and opposite reaction,"
been more true.

An online experience can be amazing, for the sake of argument let's focus on your business, your growth and your thought process.

CAN I GO OUTSIDE ; TALK to SOME·ONE ?

Take a look at a Real Estate Agent

In recent years Real Estate Agent's have really embraced Facebook. Let's think about the premise of Facebook from the consumer's point of view. Many people view it as a way to connect or reconnect with people on a social level. While the intent of Facebook may have started with that plan, the Facebook that we have all come to know as of this writing as a company has become more valuable than Wal Mart, the largest company in the country, if not the world. Clearly Facebook is not just for friends to communicate, and the Real Estate Agent for the most part has started to realize this.

Many build their business brick by brick either by the city, community or neighborhood they live in and have successfully done so for many years.

In recent years many Real Estate Agents have embraced Facebook as a model to share information with their community. The early adapters are regularly posting their listings, community events or congratulations to their clients and other vendors who were all involved in a specific sale or transaction. Clearly, this is a great source with which they have enhanced their hand significan'tly.

Make no mistake about the direction I am going, it is not my intent to tell you which social network is right for you, nor am I going to spend any time mechanically educating you on Facebook, LinkedIn, Twitter, etc. There are plenty of free online tutorials through YouTube or other video channels, and as you should be aware there are plenty of books for that. My job is to help you figure out the best way that works for you in the Networking arena.

Keep in mind, at the start of the book let's call it Networking 101, you need to figure out how to help somebody with something they need. You will feel good about it, and you will be rewarded just as a matter of fact. When you get rewarded and how you get rewarded is a whole different discussion.

Hopefully, as a Real Estate Agent you are posting your properties already, and if so, a few key reasons why it makes sense:

1. Why wouldn't you, it's free advertising.
2. You are giving people something to talk about.
   a. Let's face it we live in a world of real housewives, flipping out, DIY, who doesn't want to know what is going on next door?
3. You might find a buyer or a seller for the next property.
4. Most of us expect the Real Estate Agent to have the scoop.

You are a staple on the ground level for the chili cook off, V Day event, Christmas event, new company openings, etc.

So, now let's say you are able to handle the above on Facebook with no problem or you just understand the basics of Facebook, have an account and have done enough tooling around to have found a few friends, a few pages to LIKE and are ready to grow your network.

One of the first things I see as a prerequisite to your success is to find other service providers or retail businesses in your area that you like, and LIKE their web pages. Depending on the type of business and their growth plans and online presence you may even get a LIKE back. Remember a LIKE back is not the goal, it is a Byproduct of what you are trying to accomplish.

Next step, you have LIKED their page and now comes the Networking homework.

Scroll through their Facebook page and seek out their web page.

1. Find out what is important to them.
2. Find out what events and people they are following.
3. Find out who else you know may LIKE their page.
4. Figure out if you have common interests….in the community, hobbies, charity, etc.

Now, that you have done all this research, if they have a sale, or event coming up and you think there may be value to your friends or followers, then what you do next instantly puts you into their game. You can now get a seat at their table.

You take the most recent post that you think has the greatest value to them, hopefully you see it as a good thing and embrace it as if your own. You share that post within your community, which may also include other social networks, we just happen to be using Facebook as the main focus for my Real Estate Agents audience.

Once you share that post, two things happen:

1. You have now helped someone with something important to them.
2. They know you shared their information because they will receive a notification that you shared their information.

YOU'VE just changed the game.

Clearly you or I can't control their actions or reaction to this kind gesture on your part, but if you use some of the other skills I've thrown out in this book, such as follow up, etc., you have just created the start of your first online networking experience.

If you have still not been added or followed by this local business, you follow up the best way you can. One option is to post a comment on their Facebook post. Whatever words make you the most comfortable and are your words in your style should work. I would say something like, "Hey so and so, I really like what you guys are doing for the XYZ event, I shared it with all my clients and friends, good luck, and I wish you great success, let me know if I can do anything else to help you with this great cause."

It should not only warrant a response, but in addition should open the door for the start of what could be a great business or personal relationship.

If there is still time, a couple days or a day reminder that you can send out, please do so, none of it can hurt. Now, it's after the event, it should become your goal to see how the event went. How was the experience overall and if it went well. Keep in mind, that the reason I stressed earlier for you to find an event or purpose they are doing that you believe in, you really need to enjoy the experience and hope it evolves naturally because even while you are creating this relationship for gain you should enjoy it and want it to become a mutually beneficial one.

Once you have a taste of someone else having success because of you or your involvement it is hard to stop sharing the energy.

For Facebook Networking 101, at the very least, know the following:

1. Your audience.
2. What their needs are not related to housing.
3. Who is in their sphere of influence?
4. What attracts you to them or their business?
5. What you hope to accomplish besides the direct business transaction. (be honest, it's ok if there isn't one)

How do you use Twitter to Network?

Twitter only gives you 140 characters to describe who you are, what you do, and how you do it. There are those people that are constantly mastering the "all about them" process on Twitter, and for the record there are plenty of books on how to use social media, so hopefully you will choose one if you see a fit with your larger business model. With that said, our discussion about Twitter relates to Networking. I've regularly talked about helping others, Twitter is no exception. Informing your followers about others, their greatness, their business specials, and community events makes more sense for you than telling people who you are and how great you are. Let's face it, I have never seen a tweet on Twitter that says, "Don't use me or buy my products, I am awful." No, our tweets are all good about our wares and us.

In order to network efficiently through Twitter you need to point out what excites you about the product or service someone else is offering, you need to embrace wanting to help them get business or awareness. Of course, while it would be great if you had any amazing number of followers that is not necessarily as important as the function you just performed. You, see once you post or share an event from someone else's Twitter feed, the next time they log in to Twitter they will see that you shared their information, and hopefully the information you shared is for someone you want to help or eventually grow, continue or form a relationship with. Again, as in most areas throughout this book, the key to success is the follow up. Seeing how the game is going for others is key to you staying top of mind for them.

Remember with Twitter you only have 140 characters or letters to write your masterpiece. You need to be conscious of what message you are trying to get out there, concise and clear about how well you inform your followers. Before posting someone else's information you should also read beyond their initial Twitter feed. You should go through their Twitter feed to see what types of things they are regularly tweeting about. Also, you should see if they are a giver, see if there is someone or something they tweet about that is not in their best interest. Really what you are looking to do is truly find the essence of them and make them appreciate that you have invested your time in their success. These are also people you may want to learn more about; because clearly it is important to the person you are trying to connect with, which makes it important to you.

If you are on Twitter, Tweet me @JeffKleid and share with me in 140 characters or less one thing you have learned about Networking so far.

Over the last several months I embraced Pinterest for our business model. When I originally told my partner John that we needed to focus on this, his first reaction was, Why? My response, I don't know, but I know we need to. I am glad I did, it is definitely a social media tool to have. Just like everything else technology driven, social media and the world around it is constantly changing, so you must stay on top of it. Learning what others are doing and how they are communicating will be key as you move forward in your business and personal life.

Chapter 7

I MAY GO ALL IN

Going all in

In the late 1990s while growing my client base, I found myself getting some really difficult opportunities specific to the Sports and Entertainment Industry. The more they came, the more I questioned why they were coming in.

Clearly in a place like Los Angeles you would think that Entertainment insurance brokers would be all over the place. Well, in reality there were only a few key insurance agencies specializing in this unique space. So the fact that people started reaching out to me for these difficult insurance needs told me there was a new opportunity in an existing marketplace.

By the early 2000s using my network of business professionals and personal relationships I set out to create an Elite team of Insurance Professionals that could help me accommodate these needs. I reached out to many of the CPA's, Attorneys, consultants and Financial and Wealth Advisors I knew or was referred to by another source. Rather than directly ask them to give me business or refer me to someone to get business, I asked the following questions:

> *Who do you use or like?*
> *What do you like about them?*
> *What is the most amazing thing they have done for you?*
> *Do you mind if I reach out to them?*
> *Is there any way I can help you once I am on the phone with them?*

The above is important, because while I stress the importance of giving back and helping others in this book, it was now time for me to use my network to help my company grow; it was a selfish time vs. a selfless time.

Notice, I didn't try to get business, I intentionally didn't look for the negative, I was trying to find the new champions to help my cause.

I knew that in order to implement a plan to start a new division, once I found the right people they had to believe in me and our mission as a business. By going through the process I discussed, using my Network to find out who was right for us, I also found out who was wrong. Because I valued the input from my Network, I felt that in this industry the 2nd tier talent vs. top tier talent was the best way for me to accomplish my goal. The thought process was simple: if successful the people I brought in would bring in a new energy, and I would end up with both the right team and clientele. Upon hiring this team, (I held their hands). I paid these people more than they were getting, I held their hands, and made sure they had the tools they needed to succeed. You meet someone, you drill down, you focus and make them focus, you ask how you can help, you ask if there are any similarities with their clients, you ask what's important to them right now. Eventually you will know what they need. In fact, you will help them know what they need, and helping them achieve, well that is just icing on the cake.

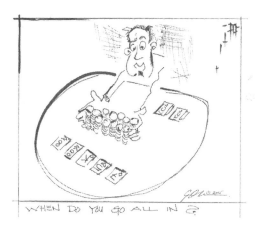

WHEN DO YOU GO ALL IN ?

Why do you need a seat at the table?

It's a good thing to know what you need when you're Networking, it is also ok to know that you do not know what you need when you're Networking. An example of this would be working in a charitable organization at whatever level they need you for, while at the same time you are trying to get a new job or start a new career. People will appreciate who you are, how you work, your commitment level, and will not necessarily count your in between status against you.

In a business-Networking environment the same traits as above may actually limit your Networking benefits. The reason for this, is that your uncertainty or in flux state may throw some people off. It's amazing how you can be the same person, but in these two diverse groups one person can be viewed by what your plans for your future are, or by the type of business you may enjoy better. Most people will not embrace your assistance through referrals or direct business. Again, you could be a great person with a great personality and story, but most people in a true business networking environment, do or should want to make sure you are fully committed to helping them accomplish their goals and having one foot in and one foot out of your business world doesn't create a great comfort level.

Just showing up gives people a better chance of working with those in the room than people who don't show up. I know it sounds simple and almost doesn't make sense, but when I say show up I mean you are showing up to every possible thing you can do with the same group of people regularly. So they see that you are involved, engaged, and have truly embraced the environment as your own. There are definitely different levels of involvement. My friend Aaron is an insurance agent who I met since I have been going to the Real Estate Broker Preview meetings. Attending broker previews makes perfect sense for me, as I am a loan officer and we also have a real estate brokerage. The broker preview meetings allow us to understand what is going on in our industry and gives us a chance to find others we can do business with and assist their clients with loans to purchase the houses. In addition to the broker preview meetings Aaron is quite involved at a board level and adds value to the industry as a whole. Of course, he is there to provide insurance to new homebuyers, as it is a requirement on most home sales. People should have insurance either way, but what Aaron does is specifically provide insurance to those people who purchase homes with mortgages. The way Aaron sets himself apart as the insurance person is his commitment to truly add value to the Association.

He started out by volunteering on an event, then another and another. Ultimately embedding himself in the environment as a person who is committed to making the association a better place.

Most recently through his involvement, he became the leader of the affiliate side of the organization down in his region and also is very involved in an annual charitable event designed to raise enough money and awareness for other members of our association if they become unable to work, disabled, etc.

Since I met him, less than two years ago, I have watched his involvement and notoriety increase, to the point that not only has he become a viable asset to the organization, but he is seeing business success as well. In fact, most recently at one of the regular meetings where he was discussing an upcoming event, another person in the room spotlighted Aaron's success in being interviewed at length in one of our trade organization magazines. While I am sure and in fact know personally that Aaron saw the opportunity to become involved as a way to grow his business, I am also sure that even he had no idea his commitment and true desire to help the organization would become so great. The only way to truly understand it and see the fruits of our labor is to keep giving of that time and understand that your commitment to the success of others and your task at hand will come back in a fashion that will make you feel good about your involvement. You need to balance it with your workload, as Aaron did, even though he didn't know just how much giving of his time would become so rewarding both personally and professionally.

Something to keep in mind, as it relates to Aaron, is that he brought to the table a unique service to the Real Estate Association as an insurance professional. He was an early adapter to the real estate space and actually paved the way for himself to get involved and become embraced easier than someone in my space. There is no shortage of residential lenders and brokers throughout the association, so our marketing approach has to be unique and different. This last bit of information doesn't take away from Aaron's hard work in getting a seat at the table, but rather serves as a side note while at the same time getting you to think outside the box as to what you may be selling or trying to accomplish through Networking for yourself. For all practical purposes Aaron may have taken a seat at the table, seen the flop, bet a bit and then realized this wasn't the right place for him. As it turned out we see that he showed up, and we also see what he did when he showed up. He created a strategy at the flop, the turn or somewhere that made him decide to go all in.

How do I make this hand work?

The follow-up is one of the most important pieces to the networking process. You can pick up cards, shake hands, say hello, and send an email to look for an opportunity. However, the follow-up is key to networking.

When you get a referral, always reach out to the person you were referred to in a timely manner. Circle back with the person who gave it to you and tell them how it went or where you stand, along with another acknowledgement for the referral. You continuously do this throughout the process of that referral. Once you understand more about the person making the referral, it will become easier for you to know how much or how little involvement they would like to have.

As a for instance the trusted advisor, coach, financial advisor or a wealth manager and in some cases different types of attorneys like to be kept in the loop and like to be able to have that conversation with the client to see how the process is going. The more informed you keep those referral sources, you add value to them championing your cause and at the same time referring you the next opportunity because of how you made them look to their client.

Chapter 8

How Do I know what level I should play at?

What is the difference between various industries and Networking groups? Networking groups come in various flavors and sizes. There are weekly groups, monthly groups, quarterly meetings, trade shows, conventions, etc., that charge you a small to high annual fee and then you may pay for breakfast or lunches weekly or monthly and they promote commerce within the group.

Business-to-Business: You are a Lender who refers a Real Estate Agent to a possible client selling their house who would be known as the consumer.

Business to Consumer: Hair Salon is the business and client is the consumer.

Blue-Collar Professionals: Makers, Contractors, Fitness professionals, Salon professionals, trades people.

White Collar Professionals: Lawyers, CPA's, CFO's for Hire, Bankers, Consultants, Marketing, Real Estate Professionals, etc.

Elevator Effect: In certain groups and organizations people come from all walks of life and with different purposes for being involved. It is as if people get off at several different floors to accomplish their goal, which may make accomplishing your networking goals harder to obtain.

The groups below include my own personal experience and in some cases goes back almost 20 years, so they may have changed the way things are done. Hopefully it will give you some guidance, but decide for yourself or reach out directly as it relates to your goals.

Chamber of commerce – Great one on one, business-to-business and business to consumer group, very localized, community driven.

LeTip – Business to business and to consumer, it was a great place for me to start, but I soon felt I was ready for another level. But with many people doing direct business with each other through self-referrals, it seemed to give me more direct business and fewer opportunities to grow my network.

Provisors – Trusted and Respected Resource group, mainly business to business and surrounded by multiple white collar service professionals, very collaborative and almost creates a suite of services from other professionals for you to assist your clients with. A large personal and financial commitment.

Entrepreneurs Organization – A business owner to business owner peer forum structure. You work closely with other business owners to tackle all types of daily long-term growth opportunities, hurdles, and plans. Good for the right business owner looking to maintain or take their business to the next level.

Industry specific organizations. Attorneys, CPA, Insurance Trade Associations - Real Estate, fitness industry, janitorial.

Miscellaneous organizations, Charitable organizations, Alumni associations, religious organizations and men's and women's groups - These organizations create an elevator effect which may accomplish your goal, but working your way through may actually be a harder task as you have to figure out what the right table is within the game.

1. Social
2. Philanthropist
3. Constant business
4. Parents told them to come
5. Looking to build network for job

There is no wrong answer, just makes it hard because everyone is getting on and off the elevator and you really have to work hard to create the right balance so you can get the response and return you are looking for. All the above are mutually exclusive good reasons, but pinpointing your audience and how to assist them makes for a difficult task. Unfortunately, this is the one area where most people feel they should start their networking world, because it seems like it would be in their comfort zone. The real take away from an organization like this should be the ability to find a mentor or a few people so you can learn more about how they got there and understand that most people are willing to embrace those discussions that involve their time if they don't feel it will have to involve their wallet.

There are additional organizations that may be for you, but I have never participated in or have direct knowledge of how to gauge them. So check them out for yourself.

Back in the game

Getting back in the game whether you need to or want to, is not always going to work out the way that you think. One of the main points of this section is to understand that people don't wait for you. Their daily business and personal lives continue on without your influence, so while you are really excited to reach out and tell them what you are up to, you have to remember and almost drill it into your head, that in order to receive value you have to add value. You need to try and learn everything they have accomplished or done since you last interacted with them. If it is a good relationship and you have established a good name and a proven track record, you should be able to get them to sit at the table with you, but it is what you do and say about your new venture or opportunity that needs to be top of mind. People don't necessarily forget about you, but they don't really stop the bus for you to get on either. Even if they embraced you in that first new interaction, keep in mind that whatever it took to get that relationship going was probably a much longer process than you are prepared for or thinking of at this moment.

You have to plan on building back your existing network, at the same time you need to start working on the new network depending on what you're doing. People age, people move on, people grow, and there are so many different reasons why it may not work this time with the same people. Don't get discouraged, there are definitely people in certain situations who get back into a space they were in or in circles they were in until they decided to stop running around in those circles and instantly, they, their products, and their business model seems to have great success. This book focuses on the rest of us, the ones who have to re-up those relationships and our building process really needs this push.

The process is very hard because now you are back in the game, playing the way you always played. The results are not happening at the same rate that they did before. You have to look back and really think about how things worked for you before. Most likely your vision of events and how they played out are very different from how they actually played out. Throughout the process of starting our new Residential Lending and real estate company, my partner regularly has had to point out and clarify some of my thoughts. When I get bogged down by what should be or always was, he will throw out a statement that basically makes me realize that there were several other variables that led to my success in certain interactions.

We take things for granted all the time. If you had a really great network of friends, and you interacted really well and for the sake of argument you just hit it off, now in the business world these people who you have a great relationship with just don't seem to be helping you with your needs and your growth process. We tend to think they will do that.

The reason it doesn't work is because people are in different stages of their life; while they might have a great desire to see you succeed they may not have the skills to make it about you. We assume that they should, but in most cases it can't and won't work. They may not have the relationships, or they may not want to because their own lives or business is all too involving for them.

I have several friends whose businesses could help facilitate my growth in the loan and real estate space. I know that their involvement will put my business in a gear that could be unstoppable, and as friends, they would do anything for me, but their entire band-with when it comes to their lives and their business is about them. I know the few things that I need from them shouldn't take up too much time, but again it is not my place to expect them to change their thought process or stop the bus to help me out. I know it's not their job to pay attention to me. Even though I want their help. It doesn't matter what their reasons are for not helping me, what does matter is that my reaction to them not helping me is consistent and respectful of our relationship. My priority should be about me just as theirs should be about them. Even when I know I have regularly added value to their lives, I can't get caught up in their thought process or even try to relate to how they view their relationship with me.

A Seat at the Table.

What can you learn?

In my case I was jumping from small blind to big Blind

Big Blind - The second forced bet in Texas Hold'em poker and other similar poker games. The big blind is generally equal to the minimum bet rounded up to the nearest chippable value

The balance between knowledge and sales is a delicate one. When you spend so much time to obtain a higher level of education to become a CPA, Attorney or MBA the energy, drive and determination you use to complete these tasks, sometimes tends to drain the marketing side of your abilities. It's not uncommon that it is difficult to excel in the sales side of this equation. In some cases your hard work and determination puts you in a job or position that intentionally limits your ability to go out and get more business.

After a year of LeTip, as I previously mentioned, I started to realize that while I had made some great friends and a few good business connections the time spent wasn't necessarily a good fit for the reward. Around the same time, my friend had been asked by a contemporary of his to join another networking group called Professionals Network Group (known as Provisors today). He told his friend who was a Partner at a large CPA practice in Los Angeles that I may be interested as well, since I was now doing more marketing for the company.

After a rigorous yet informative discussion with the CPA, he invited me to my first PNG meeting.

By now, the one thing I started to realize through my short yet adventurous time getting started in sales is that you should find out what someone is buying before you offer them something you are selling.

So, I went to my first meeting which was a far cry from the deli like restaurant with 6-8 small business owners and their employees to a conference room in a downtown Santa Monica office building with about 20 big leather chairs and middle aged men in suits greeting everyone like they had known each other forever. Oh yea, there were a couple of women too, and I say that because it truly felt like a good ol' boys network at first look.

I said my hellos and sat down, pulled out a yellow pad and pen just waiting to be a part of this thing, this amazing meeting for a guy like me with a few key accounts under my belt, barely making as much as I made as a valet at the Disneyland Hotel just a couple years before. I did it, I made the big time. Like a sponge I listened to every word from everyone and took notes, this guy was an attorney, this guy was an attorney, and this guy was a financial planner. You mean life insurance guy, right? This guy was an attorney, this guy was a consultant. A consultant, oh you mean a guy who previously worked in a corporate environment and decided to tell people how to do things? This guy was a CPA, and this woman was a commercial broker.

So there I am, a seat at the table, this is where I want to be, this is where I have to be. By the end of that first meeting I took my scribbled notes, thanked everyone I met and went out and called my wife and couldn't stop telling her what I had seen. In my mind I had just been given keys to a car, but I didn't know how to drive yet. While I don't remember exactly what were on my notes, I remember there was a point in the meeting where people talked about their needs either for themselves or their clients. By the way, when I worked at Disneyland everyone that visited were called guests not customers, and when I started in sales they were customers, but after this new amazing meeting I now had clients. I didn't know how to do it or ultimately what it would be called, but I knew even after that first meeting and the many interactions that got me to that point, that my future in both my personal and professional life would become that of a connector.

Remember how you got there.

One of the key components to getting a seat at the table is to never forget how you got there. At every step you need to keep a mental or literal checklist of the way you got to a situation, as you spend more time Networking and meeting people through the process. One thing that you start to realize is that it is a small world after all. So, when someone gets you a seat at the table you need to remember the connection, it is not only good business, it is Good Business. Sometimes you lose sight of it but it could change your opportunities. Most recently I was at a charity event-planning meeting. At the meeting I realized that not only was my good friend who brought me into the fold not there, but he was also notably left out of the task he had signed up to lead. It upset me, here I was with a seat at the table meeting nice people, finding a way to connect and help others, but still my good friend was nowhere to be found and his task was gone. He is one of the most committed guys I know; he has given his all to this group for a few years and now where was he?

So after the meeting, I took it upon myself to get in front of one of the organization's leaders. I felt an obligation to make sure my friend wasn't forgotten. I know it sounds corny, but it truly is one of the most important things you should do if you are going to be a good Networking person. You want to make sure at every turn that people know you are both thinking of them and remembering how you got there.

In addition, it is not just when things don't go right or you see something that may not seem to be ok, but at every step every chance you get, you should embrace the opportunity to touch base with a referral source or good contact. You never know where that check in can lead. Of course there are times when a good referral comes from a source that you don't connect with, it does happen and it has happened to me. It's ok, not everyone will be a great contact for life, if done correctly however you will keep and maintain many more than you don't. Most of the relationships I have had and continue to have, are because I regularly reach out just to see how they are or how I can help them.

It was interesting, the other day I had an interaction with someone my partner and I consider being an extension of our team. We were having a conversation and she was telling us about a great relationship she had forged with a prospect that is finally proceeding with a purchase for her to be involved with. While she mentioned she met him while helping us out with a program we had put in place, it wasn't until later in the conversation that I realized we had helped her eat, we had been responsible for her being able to provide for herself and her family. It's not that I needed that recognition, but rather the fact that she had no foresight or thought process to realize what we had added to her business model. She needed a spotlight shined in her face. It wasn't because I wanted the attention or the acknowledgement, it was because she needed to understand how relationships work and that we were committed to her success and not too many people that compete can make that statement or can say that statement truthfully. I Don't lose sight of the fact that her persistence and commitment to accomplishing the client's goal were definitely a key factor to making it happen, but without that interaction and us embracing her to be part of what we were doing she would not have had the opportunity with that client.

Understanding someone's Tells both good and bad.

The Tells of a Great Networker

When I talk about someone's Tells as it relates to Networking and Life, you almost have to think about it as both a positive and a negative. For example, one of the most amazing things about working at the Disneyland Hotel starting in the late 1980s was that it was a time of change, growth and maturity for both of us. At that time, Michael Eisner was the CEO of Disney and his good friend Frank Wells was second in command until Frank's untimely death a few years later in a helicopter crash. In any case, on several occasions Michael would come into the hotel and I was fortunate to be there with others waiting and ready to assist him.

What made Michael a unique person was his amazing ability to always know who you were, or at least you never saw him look at your nametag, and in every interaction regardless of how many low level managers were standing there waiting for him, he always made you feel like he remembered you and the last time you were together with him. Even in my late teens and early 20s I knew that exchange while not extraordinary, was definitely the way I wanted people to view my interactions and me.

This man had so many high level problems and still managed to communicate in a way that made you just want to create that experience for the guests. Yes, there were definitely others at that level who made you feel similar, and I could take up a couple of pages naming them all.

From the moment I realized the few unique skills from Michael Eisner, I knew paying attention to what is going on before you in any situation is a much better way of getting through life. In addition, whatever your cares, and your worries are at that moment, you need to be conscious of your surroundings and who may be affected by your

Several years later, I had now been fortunate to be President of a fairly large closely held regional insurance agency that under my direction grew significantly and since we had a significan't footprint in

the entertainment business I was at a conference called NAPTE (National Association of Producers and Television Executives) and one of the panels featured Michael Eisner and a new Webisode company he had invested in. I was just as enamored as the day I met him. Later that day, I was in a restaurant at the hotel, and there he was grabbing a quick lunch by himself. Of course, you know what I did next, yep I went up and told him who I was, and when I worked at Disney, and after he asked what I was doing now, I told him. He told me he appreciated me reaching out and that he was very excited to hear of my success and that he liked hearing stories like that. We parted ways, and I thought that was that.

Later that same day I was coming down from my room in the elevator and the guy who Eisner had invested in was riding down the elevator with me; we got to talking as I told him I was impressed with their vision. I also told him how exciting it was and what a good memory to see Mr. Eisner again, and the guy said, "Oh, that was you, Michael told me one of his old employees came up to him and he was excited about their success."

So, if there was a doubt about this man's class, or ability to make someone feel more special hopefully you will keep this little anecdote in your vest pocket, because you never know who may end up in your circle.

The Tells that help you drill down.

In order to truly focus on Networking, or constantly playing a game as I have already mentioned, you are actually playing multiple games at any time. Even if you are not focused on any specific task at hand you should be conscious of your presentation. The best example of this, at least I think for me is when I go to a restaurant, whether it's with my family, a friend, business associate or new acquaintance at any level, I am very conscious about my interaction with the host/hostess or wait staff. Most likely this comes from all my years working in the service industry whether as a busboy, waiter, valet, bellman, doorman, bouncer, Security, etc. regardless of how I know it, I am just very sensitive to my interactions in this arena.

Coming from the service business you tend to learn the different styles, intricacies, and flavors of people and we all have seen those people that don't appreciate what we do or did to take care of their needs. On a side note, I do seem to find that the people who Network most efficiently the fastest come from a background in the service business. That doesn't necessarily mean they take it to another level faster, but that their starting point seems to be at a higher level. With that said, even I don't understand when taking an order at a restaurant makes more sense without writing it down, definitely a pet peeve of mine, please write it down, managers and owners please let your servers write things down, use paper, use pen… anyway, back to the task at hand.

That interaction from you to that server truly becomes a tell on who you really are, based on who is at the table with you and how they will view you. If it's your family, clearly you want to send the right message for how they learn from you (business professional, date, etc.) Same is true about anyone else with you; I've actually gotten into this discussion with several people that surround me. I've regularly made it a point not to discuss with the person I am with at the time, but rather friends, associates and others who also understand this unique opportunity or tell you can learn from others. As I have mentioned throughout this book, sometimes you set out to meet someone or interact with someone and they, or you have a different agenda or something on their mind. Clearly when you go to a business lunch, you are hoping to do just that, business. You almost have to mentally prepare yourself for this unique interaction, I know I do. Fact is, I am regularly discussing that you shouldn't splash the pot and it's hard not to ignore when someone does that, but in this environment the server most definitely will splash the pot, but their reason is to make sure you have what you need from them. They have multiple personalities, multiple agendas and multiple thought processes to contend with so if they show up too early, they may see resistance, and if they show up too late they may see resistance -- so show up on time! Each member of the party has their own agenda. This interaction can make or break another interaction for you.

I try not to pre judge my opportunities, I have spent several years trying to be as open to opportunity and meetings as possible. At the same time, I am very big on doing homework, and peeling back the layers of a possible relationship when it seems warranted. In one specific instance, I surrounded myself with a great team of insurance professionals, whom I ultimately employed, several of them told me of their interactions with another member of their old company and they were not generally great interactions. In any case, at one point after this person left their old company he was selling a product that was new to our industry, and only he had access to it. Since I built our company and our philosophy on the "Best in Class" products and services, I had a duty to find out more about his product on behalf of my clients. You can't put yourself first. Clearly the only way to do this was to have a one on one, with a former competitor with whom several of his counterparts left to come work with me, but I needed to find out what he was selling. So we set up a lunch, more like he set up his favorite place for us to meet for lunch and we did.

Knowing what I knew, I put that in the back of my head and set out with an open mind to find out more. So now we are at lunch, sitting there, and I am using my listening skills at maximum. He couldn't have been nicer, more gregarious, just an amazing person, talked about his interests, family etc. Then it happened, the truth came out, in a matter of seconds and upcoming minutes I saw it, "The Tell" the interaction with the server, all that goodness gone in seconds and minutes. He was curt, rude, demanding, annoyed, and couldn't get back to the all about him fast enough. Everything I had heard leading up to that interaction couldn't have shown through any faster. Fortunately, his product and its concept weren't as great or unique as I was led to believe, so I wasn't so concerned anymore about the need to understand the product or his services. It is possible that me knowing more about him and his ways before the meeting may have caused me to see "The Tells" in such a clear concise way, but I think a better answer is that I am very aware of my surroundings and look at those interactions to truly understand who I am dealing with.

(His actions to the server were so much different than his actions towards me I knew immediately why I couldn't do business with this person, but I still had to understand the product)

When it's not a family member or close friends, how well you respond to that server's interaction, for the sake of argument; let's say the person you are with at lunch asks for your story. Now is your chance to shine, you have prepared for this moment, you are starting to tell the YOU story, and all of a sudden the server shows up and regardless if they jump into the mix, or stand there to jump into the mix, the YOU story has to be adjusted in the appropriate light otherwise the impression you leave will not be the greatness of YOU, but the rudeness of the REAL YOU.

Chapter 9

What can you learn from other Players?

Sometimes the game itself may not be that interesting, but what you learn from others can be priceless. I remember one day, while working at the Disneyland Hotel, working on the Drive, which was where everyone had to come to check in. It was just another busy day, typical interactions, excitement, frustration and anticipation that ran the full gamut of emotions, from both the guests and my fellow cast members. They were looking forward to the experience and for the most part we were trying to figure out whether the day was going to be a good or bad one.

I remember this van and another car coming in and running over to assist them. To my surprise, it was Henry Winkler from the show Happy Days that was popular when I was a kid. He was called the Fonze, it's ok if you don't remember, but it was a big deal at the time. Immediately, jumping out of the van and car from all sides were several kids, and Mr. Winkler calmly got out and explained it was his daughter's birthday and they were all staying overnight at the hotel. There were a few of us that helped him with all facets of getting the car, bags, checked in, etc. Even with all this chaos from his daughter and her friends, Mr. Winkler engaged us as equals; he stood around with the help engaging us for several minutes. After a few minutes he took out several $20 bills, and yes I still think that is an amazing tip even by today's standards. He took out the $20s and since he was now holding court with more people than the ones who helped him, he took the time to make sure that the right guys received the tips.

We were all pretty impressed because on several interactions with celebrities many seemed to think their presence was tip enough. The next day, when Mr. Winkler checked out he went through the same process, making sure that he personally thanked and rewarded all those involved in making his daughter's birthday an amazing experience.

I never forgot that day, and in fact, it stuck with me, it helped me understand that no matter how far along you get and how important you may be or think you are, remembering those around you is part of the experience you can't forget.

Several years after the Disneyland Hotel experience, I was playing craps at a hotel in Las Vegas on a quiet night. Up walks Mr. Winkler who asks the pit boss if it was ok if the table which was quite slow, would they lower their minimum bet so that his son who was celebrating his 21st birthday and his friends could get on and play. He didn't ask as a celebrity, he didn't demand it, what he did was ask a favor as a dad to make the experience that much better for his kid.

I stood there blown away again. By now I once again was President of a fairly large closely held Insurance Agency which had several ties to the Entertainment community and I helped grow it with every nugget I had learned along the way. In my head, I was thinking I have to tell this guy how much his interaction meant to me, but at the same time, because of working in the Entertainment space I had a great respect for public people's privacy. It was decided, I would never forgive myself if I didn't share my story with Mr. Winkler, so I did. I took a break from the game, walked over and told him about our interaction that many years before. I thanked him and his son remembered the trip well. I told Mr. Winkler, his son and friends that he and several others had helped shape and mold me into the person I had become and I thanked him for that.

What are your tells?

What kind of player do others currently perceive you as? At every step you are being sized, judged, watched and labeled. A good networker does not always mean a polished networker. Being yourself flaws and all will not limit your ability to make great long-lasting relationships. In fact, quite the opposite, we all have flaws, quirks and tells that differentiate us from the rest of the table. Embrace it and strengthen it.

You can look at image in two ways: yours and theirs. Sometimes, what seems like it should make the most sense and who makes the most sense to connect with might not be a fit for you.

I learned how to play the game the Disney way.

1. All people expect a great experience, but have different levels of what they consider to be great.
2. Helping others accomplish their goals creates an opportunity for your reward to be greater.
3. True leaders are followed and people genuinely want to be around them and their vision.
4. Managers want to be listened to, but sometimes misuse their power.
5. You never know who the person next to you is or how they may fit into your life, so don't rule them out too quick.
6. Enough random acts of kindness will definitely turn into something good for you.

How to engage in a networking situation

Board
The list of players waiting for seats at a poker room. In most groups there are people waiting or trying to meet with the person or people you are in front of. Realize that while someone may not be able to help you accomplish your goal, moving on too quickly without a proper process may be a relationship or opportunity missed...

A few things I found that worked for me,

1. See if they want to grab a coffee or lunch.
2. Ask how long they have been in the Networking group or what other groups they belong to.
3. Find out if they are going to any of the other upcoming events that you guys can connect on either side of?

Now this is where it gets tough or turns into a grey area when it comes to night time Networking groups. These are always the toughest. There are so many different types of people and not five of them will think of networking in the same light.

1. There are people who want to drink and socialize.
2. There are people who want to network at night because it

---

doesn't get in the way of their work.
3. There are people who network specifically because the event excited them.
4. There are people who just want to sell their wares.
5. Want to meet new friends and do some business.
6. There are two types of Networkers, those who truly connect people together so that everyone benefits and those that connect people with the intent that it benefits them.

Sometimes, it takes kissing a few frogs to find your match, but you can't pre judge and limit your opportunities. One of the key components to a good networker is knowing as much about your audience as possible when you know you are going to meet with them.

Whatever you do, be careful not to Splash the Pot

Splashing the Pot

Tossing chips directly into the pot. Poor etiquette.

Yes, there are those people, running through a Networking meeting, cards and flyers in hand, introducing themselves, spewing this unstoppable information about what they do, how they do it and who they can meet; yes, they still exist. And yes there is a place for in your face Networking, but even at this level there should be decorum, a process, thinking, a strategy.

Is it the right table?

Describe various Networking groups.

Differentiator between social, business, mix social and business. Goals of others, breakdown of disciplines, your goals, needs, desires, etc. Definitely not one size fits all.

What is Networking or who is in your network?

There are different groups within groups.

What products sell themselves vs. the people or companies that positioned them, what are their stories?

How many frogs do you kiss to find your flow?

Like Forest Gump said, "Life is like a box of chocolates." So true, don't rule out anything right away. Definitely ok to rule things in, but look for an opportunity to help someone.

The next person you meet may live next door to your largest future client or customer.

Genuinely wanting to help is better than faking it. Once you learn their needs depending on your network or ability to get it done you decide to move forward.

ARE YOU A POT SPLASHER? —?

The Game Changer

Many years after I left the Bell Staff of the Disneyland Hotel, I realized so many of the key defining moments which would later lead to my success. The multiple interactions with the likes of Michael Eisner, Dick Nunez and Hideo Amemiya my old boss. And other high level executives. In addition there were countless interactions with some of the most amazing people one could every meet. Whether they were executives, the CFO for Circus Circus or celebrities like Henry Winkler who showed me what true class was. All these interactions were done with a true flare for Networking.

While I have discussed many ways of interacting and many inter-actions that led to opportunities throughout my business and personal life one that stands out is a relationship that started over 15 years ago while I was involved in the insurance association. I had met a new dad in our wives' Mommy and Me class with our first son, and instantly he and I hit it off. He happened to be a CPA for people in the entertainment world. We became fast friends, and at the time business was never discussed or the issue. At one point a year or so into our friendship as I was trying to understand how to service the Entertainment community in Insurance, he introduced me to a woman named Virginia. She was a very knowledgeable seasoned insurance professional like nobody I had ever met before. She previously owned an insurance agency, but was now a consultant to the entertainment industry and trying to grow her practice. After getting together with Virginia, I knew I could help her and more importantly she could add great value to my insurance association. I had asked her to do a presentation to our insurance association. I was right, she was a hit. She picked up a few business opportunities along the way, and I am hopeful that she gained value from becoming a part of the insurance association. I embraced her for her knowledge and she embraced me for desire to learn. Over the next couple of years, regularly I would refer Virginia to consult with people and we kept the communication open. At one point a few years in to our relationship, I wanted to know what it would take to get into the Entertainment insurance space. Virginia made it very clear we would not be able to break into the space so easily. At the same time, she did share with me the same information and requirements it would take to be successful in that space.

Another year or so later, we had several of the tools we would need in place and the entertainment market had shifted and showed me an opening. Embracing that relationship, I both consulted and hired Virginia to help us enter the space. I am sure our financial commitment to her was not quite substantial in the beginning, but our commitment to not letting her down and knowledge of that was enough to help us. It was a relationship that to this day, I see as a game changing networking story, because of my willingness to give and Virginia's willingness to give. We both met in the middle, and with her help we changed the lives of many people, created a higher-level quality of life for employees, clients and our vendors for several years thereafter.

Appendix 1

TOURNAMENT PLAY

Sometimes when you understand your network, you spend so much of your time giving instead of receiving.

My move from Oak Park to Orange County was only 100 miles, but in the scheme of Los Angeles and Orange County it is sometimes considered two worlds apart. At the same time reigniting some relationships I had back in college and connecting with some prior business relationships I had between my two worlds.

I wanted a good network of people for the sole purpose of finding a good group to interact with. For the first time in my professional life it was a time, where it wasn't about growing a business, wasn't about getting an account or a sale, it was just about meeting a group of folks to connect with.

It was interesting, because for the first time I had gone into a group of about 200 Jewish men, who for the most part were there just to be there, and it was the first time in almost 15 years that I had walked into a room that large with that many people and I only knew a couple of people in the room.

It was almost surreal, I had been in many environments over the years where I didn't know a lot of people, and was trying to make connections or make business happen, but to be in a room of people in which my sole purpose was to find people to hang out with and spend some time. It was quite unique and foreign to me.

One of the most amazing things about it, was that this group was specifically a Jewish Men's group and since I was in AEPI, a Jewish Fraternity in Orange County at a University that was right next to the event I was attending, I just naturally assumed I would know more people, but I didn't, and I was genuinely both excited and nervous for the first time in years.

Almost immediately, one by one I started to meet an amazing mix of people. I met retired people, CEO's and executives from both public and private corporations, people who never really told me what they did, to people who had clearly been around, but were starting new projects, careers and companies. It was an eclectic mix of people within a group of people all there with one similarity. We were all looking to find this Jewish Community for our families and ourselves.

Over the next couple of years I really got to know several of these people really well. Through coffee, lunch or dinner events, trips, etc. I really started to learn how many different types of people could be in one group at one time.

I also learned that there were truly different categories of people involved in this group. Some folks who had seen some success founded the group. They wanted others who had seen success to share it with them as well. At the same time, what made this group unique is that for the most part, many of them were in their late thirties and into their forties and they wanted to share their excitement with their dads. I had never seen a group work this way.

Some people want to get involved in charity or philanthropy because they want to give back or they want to grow their business. In this case on its face, it seemed like the people involved truly wanted to create this environment to meet other Jewish men and be philanthropic or charitable.

It was amazing how diverse this group actually was as it related to a charitable organization, yet how they all wanted to be together. Whether it was the guy who sold his company and literally lived on the top of the hill, or the guy whose commitment was to see great things accomplished for others, via the gifts and money given through this organization. The guys who were working their way through the Jewish community. Lower, middle, higher and highest economics all in one melting pot.

I would say, genuinely 90-95% of the people were truly there to be a part of this amazing men's group and the giving back component to it. I am not sure almost six years later if those numbers are still the same. I do, however, still see an amazing energy and commitment to doing well within the space.

Even if that number has changed and the group has grown and evolved to include people looking for business or trying to grow their business, that's ok too. The catch, that is, if your involvement is solely for monetary gain, most people will figure it out and you won't enjoy the interactions as you move forward.

If on the other hand, you clearly need to grow your footprint or reach direct end user clients you need to be committed to the group. For your continued success, you need to make sure that every action you take or interaction you have involves your commitment to the success of the group and your involvement with it. Anything to the right or the left of that may hinder your success.

Understanding how to interact with others during tournament play can be quite challenging. Think about all the moving parts and the players:

1. Multiple players with their own agenda
   a. Do you understand their agenda and the different variables?
2. How do you manage your own agenda?
3. What is the cost of your involvement?
4. What do you have in common with someone?
5. How are you using your seat?

If you truly figure out the right reason to be there and are transparent about your business intentions, people who are on the high end of the spectrum, not in their wealth, but in their understanding of people, will find out who and how you really are. They will embrace you, your honesty and integrity.

THE CARDS YOU ARE DEALT !

Appendix 2

Networking in CHARITABLE ORGANIZATIONS

Its kind of funny, you wouldn't necessarily think you would have to Network or position yourself in a charitable organization to give back. Unfortunately, a couple of components come into play. One, not everybody embraces change, and you coming in, creates change. Two, not everybody that signs up for Charity work truly wants to help, they just want to see value or do it because they know other people are going to see them do it.

I have a couple of personal thoughts that hopefully will help you find the right thing to get involved with and at the same time understand why you can be in there to both do good and gain value. While this is not the take away I see from everyone, for the most part when I get involved in some type of cause that is for the greater good, when the person or people leading the group regularly express that if you are there to find business you are in the wrong place. Or they say they are only there because of the passion they have for the cause it usually puts up a flag in my head, and there is usually some truth to my concern regularly.

My approach to finding the right charitable cause, group or event to participate in is about the cause, my time, the footprint of goodness it makes and why are my skills valuable here. If you don't have cancer, and have never been affected by cancer, but you have friends who are very active in a cancer organization what level of commitment makes sense for you? If they make a good case and you feel you can add value, and gain value either by feeling good or adding to your network, you should embrace it and move forward. At the same time you should be conscious of the fact, that since you don't have a vested interest in the kicking cancer's ass, you may never see the true value of your time, even if you become a champion in the space, make a difference, and oh, by the way people may be interested in what you do in your business life, because of your commitment to seeing them succeed.

When you go to a charitable event or an organization, everybody should be coming together, but you are still judged. Getting involved in an established charity is going to give you a good footprint in understanding their history and know they are successful. The other side of that equation, is that with an established organization there are usually a handful of key people that contribute regularly and more than others, and depending on the make-up of that group it may be difficult for you to make inroads in a timeframe you would like or feel you can commit.

Networking in charitable organizations is interesting. It's kind of funny; actually, you wouldn't think that you have to prove yourself to be involved in a charitable organization. More often than not, you have to specifically, because of all the different mindsets of people sitting around the table.

When you get involved with a charitable group or organization, in theory everyone is there for the same purpose, but in reality there is quite a diverse mix of people. On the one hand you get involved with a networking group with the purpose of growing your business while helping others. As I mentioned throughout this book, you are on a level playing field as everyone is there to grow their business and hopefully add value to others. Clearly there are learning curves, different personalities, different tools that you need to accomplish these goals, but again the premise is the same. Now, let's talk charity or organizations formed with a single purpose or mission. These may be the right environments to accomplish your goals wherever they may lie on the spectrum. Charitable organizations are there whether you made your money, want to share it and make a difference, a relative had a need that could have been or was helped by this type of organization, your business model or employer requires you to participate in some kind of outreach, or you just want to stay involved with what happens in your backyard.

Regardless of your reason, now that you understand there are several different types of reasons and options for someone to be involved, you need to understand that the timeframe, the variables out of your control and the learning curve in this type of environment will be a different one than traditional Networking. Don't lose sight of it, and hopefully you will genuinely find the right organization that will allow you to accomplish your goals. For the sake of this book, we are going to assume that you know you need to grow the relationship circle of your business and your personal needs bucket. Using our example, you should and hopefully will be committed to the cause, you should be and hopefully will be committed to showing up regardless of the task that is set before you to help the organization as a whole make a difference. And just as important you should truly understand and appreciate the reach that this organization may or may not afford you in order to reach your goals. Over the years I have found several different charitable opportunities that I have either endorsed, embraced, got involved in, or passed on. I rarely make any of those decisions quickly. I invest just enough time to see where the organization is, where they are headed, what type of contribution I can make and what the organization's reach is, can be or will be.

EXERCISE

A. Describe a time when a charity made you feel like giving?

B. Now describe what types of charitable organizations would give you the same energy.

Appendix 3

Are you the Accidental Networker?
Or
Are you the Intentional Connector?

The "Cards you are Dealt" leaves the gate with a ground level education of networking. All too often the premise of Networking starts with what you have to gain, the true premise of Networking is what you have to give. How well you connect with others, learn their needs and their concerns will truly allow you to network more efficiently and connect you with those who may ultimately become your sphere of influence. Getting a seat at the table is not as important as getting a seat at the right table and the first take away in reading the "Cards you are Dealt" is that Networking is not a one size fits all process. Before you spend $25 on the next mixer or two hours in the next meeting, spend some time with the "Cards you are Dealt" and learn from an Intentional Connector what may be the best direction for you.

As previously said, getting a seat at a table is not always the hardest part in business. Finding the right table to sit at is really the key to your Networking success. Most people embrace Networking because they are told that is how to grow their network. Unfortunately, the person leading the charge has most likely seen their version of Networking work for them. In most cases they are a product of success that was accidental or right time and right place, so it doesn't truly offer the tools or skills of creating a long-term Networking strategy.

Networking for Real Estate Agents, CPA's and Lawyers

First out of the gate I find myself focusing on Real Estate Agents, they are a Group of community based, business minded individuals and very much involved in everything that they can. Real Estate Agents get involved in everything from local schools, restaurants, businesses and anywhere they can get involved, add value and be seen.

Over the last couple of years I have gained a new found respect for Real Estate Agents I have met, become friends with and regularly connect with throughout our various Networking meetings and events.

Many Real Estate Agents show perseverance that we all should, that constant positioning and churning of themselves and their products to a new group of buyers and sellers regularly. While yes, in some cases their business is quite successful, several have great referral networks, their business however, is still quite transactional.

Over the last twenty years I have regularly worked with respected and trusted advisors on behalf of themselves and their clients. I have learned the thought process and the unique desire of these advisors to hold their clients' hands and help them past the finish line on every task.

I see an amazing opportunity for the right Real Estate Agents with the willingness to adapt to a higher level of networking that may take a bit longer to mature, but will feed multiple monthly and yearly referrals. Ultimately if done correctly the right Real Estate Agents could create a consistent revenue stream in a transactional business environment. Don't misunderstand me, there are definitely Real Estate Agents who regularly get business from the same source or sources, but they seem to be the exception not the rule.

Think about it, you farm an area, why not farm the business that serves it, why not find the local insurance guy, financial advisors, lawyers, etc. Why not find these folks, serve their areas and at the same figure out what they can gain from you and your involvement with them?

CPA's

Why do CPA's and lawyers struggle so much in Networking? Both have a higher education and with that traditionally the focus has been on the classes and education, clearly in recent years.

The reality is that not everyone who goes into these professions wants to be entrepreneurial. The problem is that they spend so much time doing a good job on their profession. The problem with this is that the better they are at their craft the more they get stuck doing the time doing a good job on their profession. The problem with this is that the better they are at their craft the more they get stuck doing the work. All of the sudden they do such a great job, that their superiors embrace their success by giving them more responsibility. Ultimately they then get tasked with the opportunity to make Partner or a higher wage, but in order to do that they have to now grow their practice, the problem ensues where you have worked so hard to get noticed and be promoted, you didn't have a chance to leave your desk efficiently and learn how to network or grow your own relationships. This is quite a struggle, because now something has to give to create this balance. It is almost impossible for most people to be both a Rainmaker (a person who generates income for a business or organization) and great service provider in any discipline, but those service providers with a higher level of education struggle with it the most.

A key component to overcoming this is to create a mix between knowledge and networking as soon as you are able to. It could be as simple as going to your professional association events so that you can meet others like yourselves. These are great types of events, but you have to understand that since you are in a room of competitors and friendly adversaries there won't be any direct business to be had on the surface.

What will you learn if you drill down on friendly competitors?

> 1. What kind of attitude or energy to enjoy in others.
> 2. Who may be a good connection to grab a coffee or learn from.
> 3. All the different types of disciplines within your own field there are and who would be a good referral source for you and from you.
> 4. What vendors and resources are around your industry for you and your clients.
> 5. An association usually has a political action committee that can help you understand the landscape of your industry which will help you know more to share with your clients and place you ahead of the competition.

The next step and opportunity for networking for white collar

professionals is that most charitable organizations embrace these professionals to be involved on their boards, because it almost instantly
gives them a second pair of eyes and ears to bounce things off of. At
the same time by having these professionals on the board, a charitable
organization or foundation can save money by having professionals
giving them basically free advice as business professionals. Of course
the organizations usually outsource the actual agreements, finances,
taxes, etc. but they definitely benefit from the free labor and embrace
it.

Lawyer's

As a lawyer, you tend to go to school for a continued period of time.
You get out and you hope to find the best job possible. You land the
job, and spend a lot of time interacting with senior partners. Doing
things for these senior partners and rain makers. Your job is to help
these people facilitate the business they bring in or already have.
Eventually if you continue to perform at a level above others, at some
point you then become tasked with an opportunity to bring in business
on your own. Next step is to make partner, then you are tasked with
bringing in even more business on your own. The struggle that ensues
through this process is a fairly clear one; unfortunately it is the same
for most. What makes you move up the ladder fastest is your ability to
facilitate the business already there or brought in by others, the better you do, the higher up you go. At the same time you show success
you are now asked to take it to another level. The balance or struggle
that ensues is that between how well you service other people's business and how well you can increase your own footprint in business.
In most cases the Partners who embraced you had to build up their
networks or inherited their business from someone else. Since they
tasked you with bringing in business, it is now up to you to go out and
figure out the avenue with which that can come from.

Clearly undergraduate and graduate school programs in recent years
have embraced the need to teach beyond the books thought processes
that give you a semblance of networking or entrepreneurial acumen,
but they are still highly focused on the education for the field rather
than the interactions that will help you.

This same logic applies to CPA's, MBA's, etc. In these fields, the higher level of education is about education, testing etc. and is not necessarily balanced with the skills you will need to get ahead in your field.

So how do we accomplish this goal of getting you to the next level? Creating a balance of handling your work and networking should go hand in hand. This should allow you to prepare for the future success. The goal is to be ahead so when that time comes you will not have to be thrown into the world to perform without ongoing practice. Understand that building this network will be important to you down the road. Don't focus on what your company or its partners say you should or shouldn't do, not because they are wrong, but because they aren't you. They will never and can't ever have your best intentions or your thought process in mind. Please don't misunderstand this to say that the company you choose to work for isn't the right fit, but a simple reminder that whether you work hard and surpass goals, meet expectations or fall flat on your face every one of those options will require you to sell yourself. Those options will require you to have some sort of network to help you get to the next level. So why not incorporate the Networking process into your world now, so you can ramp it up to whatever level you need to interact with people.

The best part about having an ongoing Network even when you are not focused on Networking is that it makes it easier to insert yourself into the mix and continue down a path that forges those relationships. It may be as simple as joining your industry's association or organization. In some instances you may question how that helps you grow your business or grow your network? It's fairly simple, knowing your industry, its champions, vendors, products, and services, service providers and keeping up with recent and upcoming changes will be vital to your success. In addition, the opportunity to find out how different or similar you are to others and what is going on with others through mergers and acquisitions. It keeps your ear to the ground in a way that you will be able to reach out to your peers when you are looking for a new opportunity, new employee, new service line, and ideas for directions to bring your business. All of this is a great form of Networking. Will it get you directly to a new client? Most likely not. Will it help you understand how to position your business when you are tasked with growing your business? Most definitely so.

Focus on your growth, focus on your success. You now have proved that you can handle the work; you have to prove you can handle relationships; all these things are integral to your success. So think about it this way, if you started with all those things now after reading this chapter. You as somebody with a higher level of education, you have already mastered that balance to some semblance of success, you know how to divide and conquer your time. In this case it's ok to take your time to shore up those relationships. It's ok to work at your own pace, because you never know when you will have to increase that process. You never know, when business will fall off, you never know when you will be tasked with growing your business. You never know what change may occur with the firm or company you are at. So, the simple question would be, where do you want to be on the side of relationships, when and if something like that happens?

I remember when I was in my fraternity; I had and have a fraternity brother named Lee. I remember years after we were out of college, Lee seemed to be someone to watch for. He had built up his reputation as a feisty, honest and efficient lawyer. He worked very diligently to show success on behalf of his clients and their cases. I never needed him as an attorney, but I did know what type of fighter he was and I knew what kind of lawyer that would make him. In any case, one day over 15 years ago he called me up and said we needed to get together and go golfing. I wasn't and am still not a golfer; nevertheless I acquiesced and made a day of it.

An interesting thing happened that day, Lee informed me he was on target to make partner, but in order to do that he needed to bring in more clients. So, this speaks to this Appendix, hard worker, committed to the firm and the clients, does a great job, gets promoted, but now has to do an even better job, add a new role in order to get to the next level. On the one hand, I was honored, Lee looked to me as someone that could help him accomplish his goal. At the same time, I told him I didn't know if I had that much strength with my clients to make an introduction to a lawyer that would have any strength to make them get interested.

I told him I would do my best, he told me he had to prove his value to his organization. Tasked with this new job, I set out to find an opportunity for Lee. Lee's specialty was employment practice liability, which included defending business owners against claims for discrimination, sexual harassment and wrongful termination. Once I understood what Lee needed and exactly what he was looking for, I immediately thought of a client who was in a very fast growth mode. At the same time, I asked Lee if he could put a client on some sort of retainer, as I knew this specific client would balk at paying money for nothing. So, I brought Lee in and exactly what I thought would happen. The client expressed there was no need, but Lee just getting in front of them added value to him from the partner's eyes. Interestingly I became Lee's champion, knowing my client was growing at a fast pace, and understanding their philosophy and cowboy nature of doing things I persisted to tell them they should embrace Lee and his more than fair retainer. Ultimately, they agreed and just to take the point home even further, within a short period the client found themselves deeply in need of Lee's services, which ultimately created a significan't revenue stream to Lee and his company.

Lee and his company were quite integral to the protection of that company. Ultimately Lee made partner. Call it what you will, that relationship in college as fraternity brothers, the relationship of that we had nothing to sell, the relationship of two up and coming professionals, he asked I answered. Look at those mechanics and see that they all came together.

EXERCISE

1. What Groups or Organizations are you in?
2. Who is in your circle of influence?
3. Which person in question #2 will you reach out to first?
   a. Why?
4. Who can you can help now? And with what?

Blue collar workers – Makers, contractors, manufacturing, fitness professionals and trades people

Between directly working in the hospitality industry and handling clients in the fitness, construction, manufacturing and distribution space over the last 30 years, I have come to see a common thread in these folks as well.

The desire to be great at what they do and for the most part the passion that goes into these great industries sometimes overtakes someone's ability to sell their great products and services.

Usually, these are people who by nature are uncomfortable at Networking events, trade shows and conventions, but at the same time understand they are a must to get their business to the next level. What would be considered a simple task for a natural sales person or connector is almost lost on the person whose real art is the product they make or their understanding of why we need it.

One of the best ways to learn how to add Networking and sales to the other side of your skills is through your own trade group or association. It may seem strange to think that a room of competitors would actually be your best source for networking and learning sales. This couldn't be more true. I have been to well over 400 trade shows and conventions throughout all these years and the number of great speakers, seminars and mixers at these events has been amazing. Taking it another step further, these groups are always looking for new board and committee members to get involved. You may be reading this and shaking your head that I am wrong, you may have already gone down this road and it didn't work for you. I am not hear to say that every group works for every person, but there seems to be enough groups and industry trades out there that finding the right one using some of the exercises in this book should become a reality.

As an active member of your association or group you will set yourself up for opportunities possibly in multiple directions. Hopefully, it will also become a confidence booster as you are surrounded by people who seek you, people who want to hear about your great products and services and want to learn from you how you operate, or what you may want to learn from them. The price of admission and gaining that knowledge will be the volunteering you do throughout the year, but that same volunteering an interaction will give you more confidence and education that you can use within your local region or business circle.

1. Show up Early to an Event or a Meeting.

2. Always try and introduce yourself or say hi to the Host/Hostess, or group leader as soon as possible upon your arrival at a meeting or an event.

3. Always wear your Name Tag on the right hand side of your outfit.

4. Ask for someone's business card first, and then ask if you can give him or her one of yours. (Once you receive their card, look at it, read it, their title and where they are located, and if it is unique, let them know you appreciate that.)

5. If you are at an event with finger foods, do not eat with your right hand, save that for shaking people's hands and saying hello.

6. Firm Handshake and direct eye contact at same time.

7. No Phone once you arrive at an event, other than to schedule or find a contact to refer to someone.

8. Find out the best way to follow up with the contact you just made.

9. Always make time for a coffee.

10. Always be Interested before being Interesting.

11. Bring Plenty of Business Cards – Even if you don't like them, most people do.

12. Bring your favorite pen.

13. Bring your favorite note pad or electronic scheduler.
14. Quality of Contacts is better than Quantity of Contacts.

15. Understand that Networking is a Lifestyle, not just a sale.

Terms:

Action
Bets or betting. "There's a lot of action on this table."

The right group or the right network is one where there is a lot of action. In business, it could be direct commerce, introductions, trusted and respected advisors for clients.

Ante
A forced bet contributed by all players before cards are dealt as a way to create a pot.

The Ante holds everyone to some level of accountability; it makes you pay to play. It creates a layer of people who want to be there vs. people who may have been told to be there.

Automatic Shuffler
A mechanized box that shuffles a deck of cards.

The automated shuffler really mixes the cards so it creates a random order that they will actually go to each player. Works well with the concept in this book about the "Cards you are dealt."

Big Blind - The second forced bet in Texas Hold'em poker. The big blind is generally equal to the minimum bet rounded up to the nearest chip value.

The Big Blind is the most expensive position in Texas Hold'em, as you may end up with a bad hand that has no value, but when it is your turn to be big blind, you have an opportunity to strategically stay in the hand, ultimately you may make it to the flop and end up with a game changer.

Blocking Bet
A small bet made with the intention of preventing a larger bet from another player.

Sometimes when you take advantage of an opportunity to learn more you are rewarded for getting in first, it doesn't mean that is the right group or cause for you, it means you are open to learning more and haven't closed the door because you don't see the value for you. As a people, we appreciate when someone embraces our needs and causes or shows a willingness to learn without knowing your upside potential.

Board
The list of players waiting for seats at a poker room

In most groups there are people waiting or trying to meet with the person or people you are in front of, realize that while they may not be able to help you accomplish your goal, moving on too quickly without a proper process may be a relationship or oppor tunity missed.

Burn Card
In Texas Hold'em, the cards before the flop, turn, and river that are discarded to prevent reading of marked cards.

The curiosity of what could have been and how different cards may have changed your hand. In reality there is no value to the burn card.

Bust
To be eliminated from a tournament. To lose all your money in a cash game.

When Networking, it is definitely possible that your investment in time, energy and money can expend your resources if you are not careful, and there is no guarantee you will find success. You must gauge your success regularly.

Button
A symbol to designate which player is sitting in the dealer's posi tion.
In Texas Hold'em the dealer rotates so everybody gets to be dealer at some point. In true Networking and business groups, you need

to step up, be seen, get involved and show a willingness to do more in order to become the dealer.

Buy-In
The amount a player spends to get into a game or tournament.

When Networking the Buy-in equates to the amount of time, energy and money you are willing to spend to buy in to a group, event or interaction.

Cards Speak
The rule that your hand is the most favorable possible combination of cards, no matter how you call it.

While the cards do speak in Texas Hold'em, in Networking it is the strategy you use behind the cards and each game, which will define your success.

Cash Out
Taking your money and going home.

Sometimes, you do accomplish your goals and network correctly and you accomplish your goal. At the same time, after accomplishing your goal you may realize the relationship or direction you were going is not for you, and it is ok to move on.

Changing Gears
When a player switches his or her style of play.

Sometimes you are right on course, doing everything you are supposed to towards Networking. You work really hard to open up communication, provide a great basis for mutual success and either you or the person or group you are trying to establish an open channel with heads in a different direction.

Chop
To split a pot. Giving away an opportunity you could handle in the short run for a long-term gain.

When you think about Chopping the Pot, first thing comes to mind as it relates to business is that you are giving away money. By nature we all tend to think about that option in a bad light. How ever, if you took the same discussion about Real Estate Agents, they are regularly chopping the pot. Most try to keep the oppo nity for themselves as long as possible, but the reality is the larger the pond the more fish to catch, so other than unique property listings or unique market environments working with your competitor Real Estate Agent marketplace will help you grow your business.

Finding the right people to meet and work with is difficult, but it can be done if you go at it the same way you would go at try-ing to find a prospect or client. Understand how they sell, un derstand where their market is, and understand their clientele. If you put a small part of your sales day into understanding where and what your partners in your field are up to sharing referrals and business and thereby chopping the pot may actually help you in the long run. In a sense almost by becoming the client's confi-dante and working on their behalf to find what they need by understanding and getting to know your fellow competitors.

A little bit of a lot is much more than a lot of nothing.

Community Cards
Communal cards dealt face up in Texas Hold'em that all players can use.

Understanding the cards and how the game is played is an integral part of Networking. You should look at what the cards on the table may do for others; you have to really think about their hands to learn this.

Connected
Two sequential pocket cards. Examples: J/Q or 5/6. Every so often you align so perfectly that your future follows form with someone.

Dealer and the Button
The man or woman who handles the cards, gives out the pots, and monitors the game.

When you are sitting on the button for all practical purposes you are the dealer, all eyes are on you, the anticipation of the cards coming out and what they are, how do they land, how do they change the makeup of the game, etc. While you have no control over any of that, you truly control the board, and how you act is key to almost every interaction you will have from that point on.

Early Position
Being one of the first to act in a betting round. Usually a disadvantage.

In Networking being in Early Position is actually an advantage. You get to show up, assess and greet the host or hostess.

Fee
Money taken by the house to compensate for expenses in a poker tournament.

In the case of Networking, usually the Networking group, chamber or business group will charge a monthly or annual fee to have a seat at the table. You need to decide what your seat is worth to you and to others. You may pay for that seat and not use it and have to wait until you can stop paying to move on.

Forced Bet
Any mandatory bet, such as posting the big blind, small blind, or an ante.

The good news about a forced bet, is that everyone else at the table has a forced bet at one time or another. That forced bet may actually leave you with an opportunity that someone else may not see or may miss because they chose to get out of the hand before it gets to them, which leaves you an opportunity that otherwise you may not have taken.

Gutshot Draw
A straight draw where only one card will complete the hand.

This is the long shot, this is the type of Networking where you are committed to the game, know there may not be a good outcome, but you are committed nonetheless to see it through. Odds are definitely against you, but yes, it can happen.

Hand
The cards used by a player.

While rarely do we get dealt the same hand, the hand we get can be won or lost by the way we play it.

House
The establishment where a game is being held. It may be a casino in Las Vegas, a kitchen table, or an online casino server in an other country.

You always meet and greet the host, thank them for including you and let them know you appreciate a seat at their table. This alone may get you to the next level and help you become a welcomed guest of the house.

Image
What kind of player others currently perceive you as.

At every step you are being sized, judged, watched and labeled. A good Networker does not always mean a polished Networker. Be ing yourself flaws and all will not limit your ability to make great long-lasting relationships. In fact, quite the opposite, we all have flaws, quirks and tells that differentiate us from the rest of the table. Embrace it and strengthen it.

Jackpot
A prize fund awarded to a player who meets a set of predeter mined requirements. For example, some casinos will give a jackpot to someone who gets four-of-a-kind or higher and loses. Set your goals at what you would consider a jackpot, helping

someone with a job, bringing in a new account, increase the sale, etc.

Kicker
The remaining undeclared cards in a five-card poker hand. Sometimes you have to show all your cards and other times you can save something for later.

Limit, opposite of No Limit, No boundaries
The type of betting in a game. See No Limit, Fixed Limit, Pot Limit, and Spread Limit.

In a limit game the risk is lower, the cost of entry is usually lower. At the same time, the reward may be the same; it just may take longer to get there.

In a No Limit game, the risk is greater, you most likely will have a better group of players, and both the loss and the gain may be greater.

Made Hand
A hand to which you're drawing, or one good enough that it doesn't need to improve.

You already got what you need don't overdo it.

Marker
A promissory note or IOU, typically for a casino or gambling debt.

The times you give should be greater than the times you receive otherwise you are most likely upside down.

Middle Position
Being in between early and late position. You can learn more about the various table positions, and their impact on strategy here.

Keep in mind wherever you are in the Networking spectrum there is always someone who knows less and always someone who knows more.

Muck
To discard your hand, especially after an opponent reveals a better hand.

It's ok to start over, but make sure your cards won't work and you need to be in a different network.

Odds
The ratio between the probability for and against something happening.

In short order you will know the opportunity, you have to play through and see the turn to know where it goes, so pace yourself.

Option
The big blind's ability to check or raise in a pre-flop pot.

It is ok to invest more time, energy and money sooner than you normally would, understanding the risk versus reward will be key.

Passive
Adjective to describe a player who frequently calls and rarely bets.

Networking is all about betting on yourself, you can't wait until someone decides it is your turn to play.

Pat
A hand that you make on the flop. For instance, if you have two spades in your hand and the flop has three spades, then you've flopped a pat spade flush.

Success in spite of efforts is not uncommon, we all have it, we just have to stretch and think about when it happened.

Pay Off
To call a bet when the bettor is representing a hand that you can't beat, but the pot is sufficiently large to justify a call anyway.

There are times when you know you are out of your league and you shouldn't have a seat at the table, nonetheless win the hand.

Position
In a turn-based game like Texas Hold'em, your rank in the order of turns. This is typically categorized into early, middle, and late positions.

Everything you do in Networking or Connecting is about Positioning, but since the deal constantly rotates the only thing constant is how you consistently change.

Protect
To invest more money in a pot so blind money that you've already put in isn't 'wasted'.

Protect your investment. When Networking, your investment is time; it is the one thing that levels the playing field in that we all have the same 24 hours in a day.

Re-raise
Putting in another bet on top of a previous raise or raises.

Once you're in, you're committed and you are truly making it happen you have to take it to the end. Keep in mind that you can't control timing, you can't control others, but sticking with your plan and goal to help someone will create a return and usually a win, it just depends on where your expectations are and that they are managed expectations.

Reading
Analysis of a player based on how they play, mannerisms, and tells. Reading the room and specifically those you are trying to meet is a key component to your success. Again keep in mind, that your objective may be farthest thing from their mind, so understanding their tells is key to the success of a good Networking experience and your success in general.

Reverse Tell
Intentionally acting in a different way to give a false image.

A good thing that could come from a reverse tell, would be to downplay your accomplishments and success, while at the same time giving praise to others when it is warranted.

Rush
A winning streak

Having some success and continuing down that path can also tend to create a negative reaction, so make sure you are aware how others view your success, and what cards to show when trying to assist others with their needs.

Slow Play
To call or check despite having a really good hand. The intention is to misrepresent the hand's strength.

Or

Sandbagging
Holding back and calling despite the fact that you have a very good hand, usually to disguise strength, provoke bluffs, and to check-raise.

When my first business was firing on all cylinders it was hard not to get caught up in the mechanics of how far we had come as a company. There were definitely times where others would express to us, in a good light, how we differed from them. I regularly downplayed them, but there was an underlying energy that could not be stifled. At least by remaining grounded and not going all in, I maintained a level of relationships with almost everyone from my receptionist to the CEO's of major insurance companies.

Set
Three-of-a-kind using a pocket pair that matches a card on the board.
You have started with a good hand, and to get to the next level you

had to stay in and play, and now you may have a great hand, but you need to pay attention to the players and the table, because three-of-a-kind is not always a winner, but is a solid start.

Shill
A player who is paid an hourly rate with house money to play in games as a way to fill them up.

When you are first getting involved in a Charity or Association keep in mind you genuinely have to be there, you genuinely have to want to give of your time and make no mistake at every turn there is someone paying attention to how well you perform. While they are not necessarily put there as a Shill, they know the game and have already made their bones and won't be excited to share the spotlight if they don't believe your involvement is genuine, and quite frankly it's possible it's because theirs isn't, but they earned a seat at the table. Usually it is in the form of a competitor or someone who needs to be reminded how great he or she is, rather than embracing the fact that you are sharing of your time; even as is a by-product you grow your personal and professional fan base.

Small Blind - The first forced bet in Texas Hold'em poker and other similar poker games. The small blind is generally equal to one-half the minimum bet rounded up to the nearest chippable value. At this point, you are investing more time than others, so embrace that time to learn more about this new Network you found.

Splashing the Pot
Tossing chips directly into the pot. Poor etiquette.

Yes, there are those people, running through a networking meeting, cards and flyers in hand, introducing themselves, spewing this unstoppable information about what they do, how they do it and who they can meet, yes they still exist. And yes there is a place for in your face Networking, but even at this level there should be decorum, a process, thinking, and a strategy.

Table
The surface on which poker is played.

In the case of this book and Networking, the table is really about the people around you and the interactions you have or want to have to accomplish your Networking goals.

EXERCISES

What should you think about when finding the right network?

1. What am I trying to accomplish?
2. What am I trying to sell?
3. Who am I trying to meet?
4. What is my timeframe for making the right connection?
5. How much time do I need to spend daily, weekly, and monthly Networking?
6. Do I want to be here for myself or did someone else tell me to attend?

Helpful Hint: There is no wrong answer, but planning ahead with time, and whether or not you really want to be there will help you know which is the right group for you.

How do you follow up on a referral?

1. Reach out to the person you were referred to.
2. Reach back to the person who gave you a referral with an up date of what you have done and where you stand with the referral.
3. Make sure you continue open communication with both the person you were referred to, and whom you received the referral from.
4. If the referral source is an Attorney, CPA, Financial or Wealth Advisor traditionally they like to remain in contact with you throughout the process.

Helpful Hint: Your interactions with #4 should accelerate the relationship you are working on, and regular communication on behalf of their client or friend is one of the best ways to add value to them. In addition, you should use this time to understand how those same professionals fare with their clients so you can in turn seek out and find them opportunities that may help their businesses grow.

Think about and compare a direct sales experience with an indirect sales experience through Networking?

Direct Sales

List some reasons why the sale may not happen.

When a key person or contact leaves the company you are selling to or trying to sell to, what happens?

Give an example of when someone will not refer you to others because they don't want you working with competitors.

If a client sells their company what do you think may happen to you and your product or service?

Indirect Sales Experience Through Networking

How do you create a couple of key relationships that can bring multiple clients?

How do you obtain a larger pool of prospects?

What do you think a Champion in networking is?

How does a Champion help explain why you are the best person for the job?

Helpful Hint: A champion is someone who speaks highly of you and tells others what you do, how you do it, and why they should use you. They are basically a big cheerleader of you. What makes a Champion in Networking so important is that their allegiance to you is not dependent on the sale, rather on what you need them to do and who you need them to speak with on your behalf.

What is an Elevator pitch and how do you prepare for it?

An elevator pitch should be 30-60 seconds, and about whom you are, what you do, why you are unique and who is your target market.
Answer the questions below

1. Who are you?
2. What you do?
3. Why are you unique?
4. Who is your target market?

You should be memorable.

Helpful Hint: As long as you hit the key points above it is ok if your elevator pitch is not as polished as other people around the table.

What are your hot buttons or what excites you?

1. What hobbies do you have?
2. What type of event do you like to go to?
3. What is your average budget to get one on one with someone?
4. What type of people do you usually surround yourself with?
5. What is your favorite charity or charitable cause?

Helpful Hint: You will find that people with common likes, needs, hobbies and causes, seem to find each other easier. Finding these same people who are focused on what you are trying to accomplish still may be a process but an easier one once you know have a clear roadmap of who you are.

How will you know when to move on to a different Networking group?

1. You are not committed or not engaged.
2. You are not interested.
3. You regularly start to meetings and events.
4. When you start to feel you are better than the group, and feel you have nothing more to gain.

Helpful Hint: It is better to confront that the group is not for you, rather than make it linger. If people start to see you are not committed, stop showing up or seem like you are better than the group, that is the impression you will leave on them. A straight forward approach to leaving will keep relationships intact.

What are your strengths?

1.
2.
3.
4.

What are your weaknesses?

1.
2.
3.
4.

What are your hobbies?

1.
2.
3.
4.

What type of event do you like to go to?

1.
2.
3.
4.

*What are the different types of people you usually sur
round yourself with?*

1.

2.

3.

4.

*What are some charities or charitable causes you like
being involved in?*

1.

2.

3.

4.

Helpful Hint: Once you figure out the above, look for
commonalities that may assist you in finding a group to join, people to
meet, or a charitable cause to embrace.

LEARN | EMPOWER | INSPIRE
Yourself /Others

2♠
Short Attention span

How do you move quickly
from project
to project?

The quality of your
interaction is better than the
Quantity of interactions.

10♥
Deliberate

Who receives that value of
your purposeful interaction

An intentional interaction
is a great trait to have when
used to guide others.

- Learn, Know, and Play the Cards you were dealt?
- Learn the strategies behind Cards others were dealt.
- Great educational tool for Sales people to understand your buyers.
- Teach a child how to engage with others.
- Understanding your Cards will help build your Network and relationships.
- Each card will educate you and enhance your knowledge about others.

THE CARDS YOU ARE DEALT PLAYING CARDS

**To purchase the cards go to www.JeffKleid.com
www.TheCardsYouAreDealt.com - Podcast**

Made in the USA
San Bernardino, CA
30 June 2016